MW00626277

Praise for The Metaphysical Christian . . .

In ***The Metaphysical Christian***, Charlotte Goodwin offers a revealing account of how she has come to reconcile her bedrock Christian faith with the spiritual gifts with which she was blessed. Whatever your relationship to Christianity or the metaphysical realm, you'll find inspiration, reassurance, and wisdom in these pages.

—Nancy Carleton, Editor of Bestsellers by Dan Millman, Lynn Andrews, Don Miguel Ruiz, and Deepak Chopra

In telling her story, Charlotte shows us that Christianity and metaphysical spirituality are not at odds with each other but are noncompeting paths on this journey called living.

—Barbara Karnes, RN, End of Life Educator

The Metaphysical Christian is a superb perspective of the unity of religion and metaphysics from the viewpoint of a truly good human being.

—Lander Rodriquez, gifted artist and photographer in the commercial arts realm for over 25 years in Los Angeles, CA, Mexico City, MX, and San Miguel de Allende, MX.

The Metaphysical Christian

Also by

Charlotte McGuire Goodwin

The Twisted Path

The Metaphysical Christian

Embracing Christian Divinity and Metaphysical Spirituality

Charlotte McGuire Goodwin

Santa Fe, New Mexico

Published by: Spirits and Miracles
2 Emblem Road
Santa Fe, NM 87507
www.spiritsandmiracles.com
spiritsandmiracles@gmail.com

Editor: Ellen Kleiner
Book design: Lander Rodriquez
Front cover image: Lander Rodriguez

First Edition

Printed/Published in the United States of America

Publisher's Cataloguing-in-Publication Data
Names: Goodwin, Charlotte, author.
Title: The metaphysical Christian : embracing Christian divinity and metaphysical spirituality / Charlotte McGuire Goodwin.
Description: Identifiers: Subjects:
Santa Fe, New Mexico : Spirits and Miracles, [2020] | Includes bibliographical references. ISBN: 978-0-9798348-1-3 (Ebook) | 978-0-9798348-2-0 (POD)
LCSH: Spiritual formation. | Spiritual life--Christianity. | Metaphysics. | Self-realization. | Spiritual healing--Religious aspects--Christianity. | Mental healing--Religious aspects-- Christianity. | Psychics--Religious aspects--Christianity. | Healers--Religious aspects-- Christianity. | Spirituality. | BISAC: RELIGION / Christian Living / Spiritual Growth. | BODY, MIND & SPIRIT / Inspiration & Personal Growth. | PHILOSOPHY / Metaphysics.
Classification: LCC: BT732.5 .G66 2020 | DDC: 615.8/52--dc23
1 3 5 7 9 10 8 6 4 2

DEDICATION

To Donnie, Shane, Christy, Cari, and Paul:

You are the loves of my life and my inspiration.
Thank you for being mine.

To God, Jesus Christ, and the spirits of the Christ Light:

Thank you for providing safe shelter for my insecurities and allowing me to experience your light and your unconditional love.

CONTENTS

INTRODUCTION

How Can You Call Yourself a Christian?

I have the core Christian belief that God is the basis of all things, and Jesus Christ—the Son of God—is my Lord and Savior. Simultaneously, I believe that God blessed me with the spiritual metaphysical gifts of hearing and seeing spirits and feeling the presence of spiritual energy, so that I am a vessel used by Spirit for communicating with and healing others. This combination of having traditional Christian beliefs and possessing metaphysical gifts caused me continual conflict and fear from my childhood to adulthood, while growing up in a strict Christian home with a Southern Baptist preacher father who led me to believe that only sinners against God claim to possess such abilities.

Not until 1997, when I was fifty-one years old, did I disclose to family, friends, and the general public my involvement in metaphysical spirituality. Though I have now been a healing practitioner for twenty-two years, I am still confronted by people who feel a conflict exists between Christianity and metaphysical spirituality. People have reacted to my disclosure in a variety of ways, ranging from acceptance and polite skepticism to disgust and criticism. I've been called a witch and told I've walked with Satan. Skeptics have asked, "How is that possible? Are you making things up? How can you call yourself a Christian?"

Each incident of disbelief and skepticism I've encountered, especially since 1997, has caused me to doubt myself, question my abilities, and wonder why God chose someone like me to do his handiwork. But I have gradually come to realize that God opens the door for many to be his tools; they just have to listen and be available.

Further, I believe God chooses many people to help others understand they are allowed to combine belief in Christianity with metaphysical spirituality and that as long as their intentions come from a spiritual place they need not fear indulging their curiosity about spiritual modalities or embracing their metaphysical spiritual experiences. It is written in the Bible that it is God who guides their path to discovery:

> "Now there are varieties of gifts, but the same Spirit." *(Revised Standard Version*, 1 Cor. 12:4)

> "And there are varieties of service, but the same Lord." (1 Cor. 12:5)

"And there are varieties of working, but it is the same God who inspires them all in every one." (1 Cor. 12:6)

In the early stages of my development as a spiritual healer, I questioned the validly of my experiences and abilities and thought perhaps I was fantasizing. Now, after years of self-discovery, I can say emphatically, "I am a metaphysical Christian," the term I use to define my combined religious and metaphysical spiritual beliefs. Although arduous at times, the last twenty-two years have given me the confidence and comfort to embrace my spiritual evolution and still stay true to my core Christian belief in God and Jesus Christ. I have navigated the melding of my Christian beliefs and metaphysical gifts through conversations with God, Jesus, and spirits of the Christ Light.

I am neither a religious scholar nor a philosopher. This book is not intended to challenge the Bible or any other religious tenet. I have written this book because I have been approached time and time again with the same questions with which I personally grappled during childhood and adulthood: "Will God be vengeful if I seek guidance or healing from a spiritual practitioner? Will I be condemned to hell if I have metaphysical experiences or gifts?"

Wondering if I was an anomaly because I believed in Christianity and metaphysical spirituality simultaneously, I emailed a survey to people I already knew and people I didn't know but whose contact information I had, hoping to find out what others thought about combining beliefs in organized religion and metaphysical spirituality.

To me, the most important questions in the survey, along with their responses, were the following:

- Were you raised in a strong Christian environment?

The overwhelming response was "yes!" The people who said "no" practiced their faith on a regular basis. Only one claimed to be an atheist.

- Have you personally had a psychic, spiritual, metaphysical, or paranormal experience?

Sixty-three percent answered "yes." Some described many episodes in detail, and others said there were too many to count.

- Do you believe there are people who can see, hear, feel, and communicate with the spirit world?

Eighty-four percent said "yes." Some even said they had communicated with the spirit world.

- Do you feel the Bible is the total truth?

Ninety percent said they believed in the possibility of mistranslations. The major opinion was that the Bible had been written by man for man and translated many times into different languages and that numerous books in the Bible had been deleted for various reasons, so the Bible was not the absolute truth but, being an old document, must contain many truths and be divinely inspired.

There were people who shared their fear about asking for a spiritual or psychic reading or an energy healing because their religion considered this a sin. Others had had metaphysical experiences but were afraid to tell anyone about them.

I was surprised by the outcome of this research. It suggested that many people are open to metaphysical spiritual principles and practices but need an explanation of their compatibility with organized religion. Overall, the survey reinforced my own simultaneous beliefs in Christianity and metaphysical phenomena, as well as the responsibility I felt to write *The Metaphysical Christian*.

My primary purpose in writing this book is to offer understanding and comfort to those who have traditional religious beliefs and are concerned about learning about or engaging with metaphysical spirituality. I hope to reassure people who feel a conflict between religious teachings and metaphysical spirituality that it is okay with God to believe in and practice both simultaneously for God encompasses all spiritual activities in his name. Another purpose of this book is to help those who have family and friends with metaphysical gifts better understand and appreciate that God embraces the ones to whom he has given these gifts and experiences.

The Metaphysical Christian seeks to bridge the divide between embracing Christian divinity and embracing metaphysical spirituality, revealing the teachings of God's angels and spiritual messengers that all religions walk hand in hand with metaphysical spirituality and that no one need be afraid of such a path.

CHAPTER 1

Early Encounters with Spiritual Contradictions

My parents believed in attending church on Sunday mornings, Sunday nights, and Wednesday evenings. I sat in the congregation at a young age listening to the preacher's sermons. Most of the time I had no idea of their meaning, but occasionally I understood the word sin and the phrase born with sin, both also used by my father. As I grew in age and understanding, I learned that Baptists believed children are born with original sin, so in my mind, the preacher and my father thought I had been a sinner since birth. At the age of six, without my full understanding of how I had been sinful, my father insisted I be baptized so I could be saved. Too young to go against anything taught by my father or the church, I complied. In retrospect, I believe that this is when I first began to question the reasoning of the church and my father, wondering how I could be a sinner as I was just a little girl.

Similarly, my husband has expressed dismay with the Catholic Church's teaching that all children are born with original sin, telling me, "When I was a child, my parents made me go to confession every week. I didn't know what to say to the priest, because I didn't know how I had sinned. I made things up to confess."

In researching the concept of original sin in the Bible, I came across what appear to be two contradictory verses:

> "Behold, I was brought forth in iniquity, and in sin did my mother conceive me." *(Revised Standard Version*, Ps. 51:5)

> "The soul that sins shall die. The son shall not suffer for the iniquity of the father, nor the father suffer for the iniquity of the son; the righteousness of the righteous shall be upon himself, and the wickedness of the wicked shall be upon himself." (Ezek. 18:20)

The first verse says people have original sin at conception; the second one indicates that people do not inherit the sins of their parents or vice versa. Considering the seemingly contradictory teachings, it is no wonder that people are confused by the Bible-based teachings of the church. Confusion and contradictions regarding religious teachings led me to question the beliefs of organized religion early in life before I had heard of metaphysical spirituality. Not until I was an adult did I know that my experiences of spirituality were different from those of most individuals and I needed answers that organized religion couldn't give me.

Fearing I would be ridiculed and knowing she wouldn't believe me, I never divulged my metaphysical experiences during childhood to my mother, who came from a devout Christian family. Consequently, she had no idea that the imaginary children with whom I often played weren't imaginary but spirits.

My father seemed to notice that I had unusual awareness as a child, though we never discussed it. I remember going with him on business appointments. Others gave me the nickname Mac's Shadow because I was always by his side. Too young at age four to comprehend his reason, I eventually learned he wanted me to meet his prospective business partners because of my intuitive abilities. One day I heard him say, "If Charlotte doesn't like them, I don't want to do business with them. She has an uncanny knowing of people's intentions before I do." He never asked or discussed with me what I knew or how I knew it, perhaps just accepting my ability as a child's intuition.

Much later, when my mother visited me at my home in California in 1999 for Christmas she confirmed for me my early gifts for metaphysical experiences. Before time for her return to Dallas, she became ill and I took her to my doctor. Upon his advice, she stayed in California in my care until she felt well enough to travel. Her extended stay gave us time to explore a subject about which I had many questions: her childhood and life before my birth.

One afternoon while she rested and I sat in a chair by her bed she spoke about the day of my birth, describing how on that day in early July in Lawton, Oklahoma, it was windy and 114 degrees, conditions that added to the discomfort of her pregnancy. When she went into labor, her older sister drove her to the hospital. In the early morning of July 7, 1946, she gave birth to me. When she and my father knew I was a girl, the previously chosen name of Charles Thomas McGuire became Charlotte Ann McGuire. Five days later my mother and I, both deemed healthy, were released from the hospital.

I had always had an uncanny memory of leaving the hospital that day, and now shared the vivid vision I'd had most of my life with my mother, saying, "I remember someone carrying me down a brightly lit hallway toward a large set of double doors. I saw the person's arm jut outward and push one of the doors open, allowing us to exit the building. Once outside, the person holding me stood on a cement landing bordered on two sides by tall evergreen shrubs. I saw a flight of concrete steps with a dark handrail. Rather than descending the steps to the sidewalk and street below, the person continued to stand on the landing. The brightness of the sun made me squint, but I looked at the enormous blue sky for the first time."

"That's right!" she confirmed. "But how did you know? Babies don't have the ability to remember those kinds of things."

Mother's confirmation of my vision gave me great reassurance about the truth of my early experiences. I had long questioned the validity, and now I knew that my extraordinary experiences of awareness had begun shortly after my birth. But my mother's question about how I knew made me uneasy about potentially being accused of having gifts she regarded as a sin against God. How could I explain to her, a devout Christian, that Spirit had shown me a "video" of that day? I wondered. Fortunately, she was too tired at the time to ask for further explanation.

Looking back on that conversation, I've often wondered how I would have answered if Mother had persisted with her questions about my ability to see such a vision. It was still too early in my spiritual development to be able to explain how I could worship my Christian God and yet be privy to metaphysical spiritual experiences. That day I realized that I could not open my mother's mind to belief in these incidents. It was apparent that due to her devout Christian upbringing the door to other wisdoms would remain closed.

Only later in my spiritual development did my relationship with God and Jesus Christ change from one of fear of condemnation to one of unconditional love, and I learned from the teachings of spirits that the gifts bestowed on me as a child did not make me a sinner, that babies are not born with original sin. Thus my childhood concerns about being born a sinner and being a sinner as a child were laid to rest, and I was given reassurance of God's acceptance for possessing metaphysical gifts.

CHAPTER 2

Facing Religious Conflicts and Embracing Spiritual Gifts

Even as a child I recognized contradictions between the teachings of my Christian upbringing and the behavior I observed of so-called men of God. The belief I had that pastors who represented themselves as holy men were supposed to not only teach the way of God but live it in their daily lives often conflicted with what I witnessed.

The contradictions that influenced my life the most in my younger years and into adulthood concerned morality, in particular contradictions between religious tenets my father taught and his own behavior. Observing my father's actions, I noticed early on that he sometimes appeared to be two different people—one religiously inclined and one abusive toward my mother and our animals.

A tumultuous relationship existed between my father and mother throughout my life. During my childhood, unspeakable things occurred between them that invariably caught me in the middle. Due to the ups and downs in their relationship, they lived together, then separated, then repeated the pattern all over again. I don't remember a holiday when my mother didn't accuse my father of an extramarital affair. I don't remember a holiday when arguments didn't result in violent hitting by both parents. I don't remember a holiday when I didn't hide behind doors or chairs to escape their fights.

When I was young, I didn't realize how my father was being abusive to me when he told me of bogeymen hiding under the bed waiting to grab my ankles if I attempted to get up; when he spanked me hard, making it difficult to breathe; or when he, in my presence, hit my mother or beat our dogs if they barked. I lived in a confusing environment with no explanation of how his behavior conflicted with his Christian beliefs other than his instructions to "believe in God and do as I say."

When my father behaved as a godly man, he read the Bible aloud; told me stories about Jesus; urged me to live as a Christian differentiating between good and evil, right and wrong; and taught me about guilt, especially associated with not living a Christian life, warning me of going to hell if I lived in a manner contrary to our religious beliefs and teachings. However, my father didn't teach me how a Baptist preacher and strict follower of God could beat my mother and the animals, or terrify me with horror stories about bogeymen, or allow me to witness his abuse of my mother. The glaring contradictions between my religious teachings and daily family life caused me continual confusion and stress. Both my parents proclaimed to be devout Christians, both proclaimed to love the other, and both proclaimed to love me, especially my father, but their actions did not reflect these claims.

One incident revealing moral contradiction occurred at a Sunday evening church service in Shreveport, Louisiana, when I was eleven. At the conclusion of the sermon, the choir sang the usual invitational hymn, and the pastor invited those who felt God's calling to walk down the aisle and join him at the front of the sanctuary. Since I had been baptized and saved, I felt no need to join him. A man dressed in dirty, ragged clothing entered the sanctuary through a side door, removed his worn-out hat, bowed his head, and slowly approached the pastor. The pastor ignored the man's presence, leaving him standing alone for several awkward moments. The assistant pastor finally spoke with the man briefly, without extending his hand to welcome him. The despondency in the man's face as he stepped back and slipped out the door was evident to me. I felt despair in my heart—the man's despair—knowing it had taken courage for him to enter the sanctuary and that he needed to be in the presence of God and his followers. I cried, wanting to run after the man and throw my arms around him.

Instead, I sat quietly and questioned the pastor's motive for turning the man away. Often his sermons had referenced God's love for all his children. Was the man not one of his children? I asked myself. I felt that the pastor had acted contrary to what I had been taught about God's love. Upset and confused by the pastor's behavior, I decided that the God I worshiped and trusted had no representation that evening. That God loved everyone the same and didn't choose who to love based on clothing and circumstances. But the God I saw represented by his disciple the pastor, only loved particular people at particular times. I went home struggling with the conflict I had witnessed, concluding that my idea of God was different. Thereafter, I no longer took to heart Sunday school lessons, for I had seen a powerful man of God turn away a poor soul. I resolved that if the church's God allowed such a moral contradiction to exist, that was not my God.

In years to come, I continued to be confused by the religious and spiritual contradictions evidenced both in church and in the behaviors of men and women in whom I once had had faith. I also wondered about potential contradictions between church teachings and unusual spiritual episodes I witnessed, knowing that according to Christian teachings incidents of this kind didn't occur except with God and Jesus. A story my father had told me when I was growing up added to my confusion about these conflicting beliefs. He related how he had experienced a visitation from Christ when he had been living in Hollywood, California, working as a blackface comedian in the movie industry. "I was walking down the street in Hollywood after a day of filming at the movie studio," he had said. "All of a sudden, Christ appeared on the sidewalk in front of me. Christ told me to go back to Texas and become a preacher. I paid attention. I quit the movie business, gave up my radio show, and returned to Texas to begin my studies."

"Christ talked to you?" I asked, hoping to hear further details about his miraculous experience.

"Yes. And that visitation was very special," he said. "It changed my life."

I felt the story about my father's visitation from Christ was very special, but confusion about its implications soon replaced my excitement. My father, a traditional Christian man, had now told me he had seen a spirit, while previously he had taught that ordinary people don't have such experiences, that they only happened in the days of the Bible, or that Satan attempts to control and use people by making them believe an angel is speaking to them. My father seeing and hearing Christ certainly contradicted everything I'd been taught.

On the one hand, the story raised more questions about my increasing confusion between Christianity and spirituality. On the other hand, it gave me hope that I might not be too different after all, that maybe having unusual experiences didn't make me a sinner. If my father, who professed devout Christianity, could see and hear the spirit of Christ, maybe I could see the occasional spirit and still be a good Christian, I thought.

Yet because at the time I didn't understand the meaning of seeing or hearing spirits and ghosts—having a father who never spoke about such encounters except the one vision of Christ, for fear of being damned to hell or ridiculed by my family—I continued to keep my own "visitations" from spirits secret. Only years later, after moving to Dallas, Texas, and living in my brother's house did I finally admit to seeing spirits.

The first time I admitted to myself or anyone else that I could see spirits was one day in junior high school when I told Jan Smith, my best friend and confidant, who never seemed judgmental, that I had seen a woman standing in the hallway between my mother's room and mine. Jan appeared a little anxious as I described the spirit's appearance. "It's okay, Jan," I said. "It's not the first time I've seen such things, though I haven't told anyone about my experiences." I had felt courageous telling Jan, someone raised in a very religious family.

Though I had longed to speak to others of this ability, disclosure of my gifts to anyone other than Jan did not seem an option since, living in a Christian family, I feared that I would be chastised, perhaps disowned. Consequently, the conflict of being a Christian yet having the ability to see spirits still raged inside me for a long time thereafter. All the while, I felt that surely my God wouldn't condemn me to hell for something I couldn't control.

While growing up, I didn't have sufficient guidance about my gifts. My father's limited presence in the home never allowed much time for personal conversations, especially involving questions of the soul. If I had had more guidance when my spiritual gifts were surfacing in early childhood, I feel I would have better understood them and grown up less confused. Perhaps I could have asked my father if, in addition to the vision of Christ he had seen in Hollywood, he had seen other spirits during his lifetime, but I didn't feel this was possible given our tentative relationship. Since then I've wondered whether, if he had the gift of seeing spirits, he also felt inner conflicts concerning Christianity and metaphysical spirituality. I wondered if customary denial that metaphysical encounters occur in modern life allowed him to avoid similar conflicts.

My father died when I was thirty years old, before I revealed my gifts publicly at age fifty-one. The only conversations I had with him concerning spiritual gifts took place after his death, when his spirit visited me and assured me of the understanding he now had of the spirit world and of my gifts and metaphysical spiritual experiences. Although I greatly appreciated his revelations and support of my spiritual journey, it would have given me great consolation to have shared my secrets with him during his life on earth.

CHAPTER 3

Seeking Spiritual Refuge and Protection

Being overwhelmed by the moral and religious contradictions I had witnessed during my childhood led me to increasingly seek refuge in spiritual experience as protection. This pattern became especially apparent to me as my devout Christian parents continued their un-Christian abusive behavior toward each other, with me as a witness. I knew from conversations with friends that other parents fought but attempted to hide their confrontations, not wanting to scare their children, while my parents used no such discretion, my mother continually telling me about my father's infidelity, complete with the lurid details. Although I believed Baptist teachings that God takes care of his children, it still didn't ease the pain of witnessing these encounters or the fear that one of my parents would be injured during their constant fighting.

As one way of coping with my conflicts and fears, I began to travel out of my body to safer places. While lying in bed one night when I was about eight years old, I felt an unusual sensation of rising out of my physical body then descending to a beautiful serene place, where I watched animals romping in fields of green grass and flowers swaying in the breeze, and heard children's laughter breaking the silence of a still summer day. Their innocence and carefree attitude as they played gave me a feeling of calmness and relief. Afterward, I felt myself descending back into my physical body then easing into a restful sleep. I was too young to realize that the out-of-body travel was an ability God had given me for my protection, a method of taking refuge from the tumultuous interactions between my parents.

My out-of-body travel continued as I grew up even though I had no conscious understanding of, or explanation for, the experiences. When they happened, I felt such emotional relief that I was able to push any questions concerning the religious and metaphysical contradictions out of my mind. Then one fateful day when I was thirteen the comfort I had gained from the belief that God was protecting me abruptly ceased due to a traumatic experience involving the acrimony of my parents.

My father was scheduled to go to Shreveport on a business trip. When my mother asked if she and I could join him, he said, "I'll be too busy, and y'all will be bored." Suspicious of his attitude from years of enduring deceit, my mother decided to drive to Shreveport with me the following Saturday to pay my father a surprise visit. After arriving at my father's hotel room and waiting while the bellboy knocked several times on the door with no response, my mother told him to use the key. Before the bellboy could turn the key in the lock, my father peeked out the door, his hair disheveled, and said, "Peggy! Just a minute. Let me get dressed."

As my father attempted to close the door, my mother pushed inside and he stumbled backward. Confused, I stood in the hallway with the speechless bellboy and watched my naked father rush toward the far end of the bed and reach for his glasses from the bedside table. I saw my mother hit him in the face with her fist, knocking his glasses to the floor.

"Charlotte!" she screamed. "Come in here and see what he's doing! He and this woman are in bed together. I knew she'd be here."

My mother's words exploded in my ears like a cannon. I stared through the open door with my hands clasped tightly against my chest, unable to utter a sound.

"Charlotte, I said come in here!" my mother again shouted.

Afraid not to obey her angry command, I stepped inside the room. A naked, blonde-haired woman rounded the corner from the bathroom, carrying her clothing in her hands, and said, "I'm so sorry," as she rushed past me and out of the room.

My mother continued to rage at my father, who tried desperately to get past her to his robe to cover himself.

I looked, but I didn't see. I listened, but I didn't hear. My consciousness floated upward from my body toward the ceiling, where it hovered over the hotel room. I felt as if I were merely watching actors on a stage from high up in a gallery, no longer able to feel the emotional turmoil caused by my parents standing below. I have no recollection of the events that followed. I only remember my consciousness returning to my physical body the next day while sitting on a bed in a different hotel room, where I listened to my mother and father argue about his infidelity.

At thirteen, I felt my world had been shattered. I wondered how my father, whom I believed to be a devout Christian, could act so sinfully and how my mother, an equally devout Christian, could lead me into such a den of iniquity rather than protect me from his displays of infidelity. And I wondered how my loving God, whom I trusted with every fiber of my being, could allow me to suffer by witnessing such a horrific and despicable incident.

As a result, I temporarily lost my belief in the Christian teaching that God would always love and protect me. For several years, I thought perhaps God didn't exist or no longer loved me the way I had been taught. I felt I had been betrayed by all who claimed to be holy. In that one day, I lost my faith in my father, the one man of God on whom I thought I could count; I lost my faith in my mother, who, by taking me along on such a horrific journey, had betrayed my trust; I lost my faith that God would protect me; and I lost my childhood innocence.

Countless children and teenagers, as well as adults, have been abused or witnessed abusive events. These experiences cause an inner devastation that takes an enormous toll on the victims. To escape the pain some commit suicide, others take on multiple personalities, and still others turn to prostitution or crime. During abusive episodes between my parents, as a child and later as a teenager I escaped via God's gift of a metaphysical ability to leave my body and travel to more carefree and loving environments, where my heart was filled with joy. In retrospect, I also believe that out-of-body travel, as well as my ability to see spirits, demonstrated God's ongoing reassurance that I could have metaphysical spiritual gifts and still retain my core Christian beliefs, easing my fear of sinning against God and making me feel optimistic that I could meld the two beliefs as a foundation for later helping others better understand their own gifts or heal from trauma.

CHAPTER 4

Metaphysical Spirituality as Sanctioned by God

For three years after the incident in Shreveport, my religious beliefs remained in no man's land. The event left me devoid of any feeling of concern about God's love and protection. Deep in my soul I still loved God, but I didn't understand how he could allow me to be in such abusive situations. Although hurt beyond comprehension, I felt no hatred in my heart—only tremendous sadness and loneliness.

In hopes of restoring my faith in Christianity, during one summer vacation in high school I read the entire Bible. But it didn't help. The loss of my faith also impacted the conflict I felt between Christianity and metaphysical spirituality. Any metaphysical experiences I had, though few and far between, I ignored, closing my mind toward both religion and metaphysical experiences. I didn't think about God. I simply lived each day as a shallow teenager who only cared about teenage friends and activities.

My relationship with my father never regained the same stability and closeness as when I was growing up. Believing he was no longer worthy of the respect I had shown him in the past, I now considered him to be just a man who drifted in and out of my life. My mother and father reconciled, split up, and reconciled again. During the short periods of reconciliation, I had to obey my father's demands and rules, but, though still I loved him, I no longer saw him as the man of God I had perceived during my childhood.

My parents' on again, off again marriage finally resulted in our family moving to Fort Worth, Texas, for new jobs and a fresh start. After the move, we attended a small church for a little while, and, upon request from the pastor, my father even preached at a revival. His hellfire-and-damnation sermons moved many of the attendees to their knees during the invitational hymns, and I stared at all of them with resentment and disgust.

A few months later he insisted we join a large Baptist church with the typical Sunday morning and Sunday and Wednesday evening services. He made me attend every service, but I didn't care much about anything that had to do with church, though I joined the choir because I loved to sing, which made the required attendance tolerable. There were many week-long revivals as well, when my father made me attend services every night. These nights would have been pure drudgery were it not for interactions with friends.

During one revival, an unforgettable event transpired that, surprisingly, helped me regain my lost faith in Christianity. After the sermon, to which I had paid no attention, had ended, the pastor asked the choir to sing the invitational hymn. He stepped down from behind the pulpit to the floor of the sanctuary, where I could no longer see him, but the microphone continued to amplify his voice as he said, "Won't you join me down here and show God how much you love him? He gave his only Son to die for you. Christ died so you could live. Believe in the Lord Jesus Christ and you will be saved."

The congregation stood as the choir sang "Just as I Am," one of my father's favorite hymns, composed by Charlotte Elliot, after whom I had been named. Growing up with one of the best hellfire-and-damnation preachers around, I had sung it all my life. This time, however, something was different. My heart rate accelerated, a feeling of sadness rose from my chest to my throat, and I began to feel guilty for questioning God's love. Then I felt myself step from the pew out into the aisle and walk toward the front of the church, as if propelled by an unknown force. As I approached the front of the sanctuary, the pastor extended his hand toward me and said, "Bless you, child. Let us kneel and pray." He then led me a few steps away to the first row of pews, gestured me to kneel, and prayed.

At that moment, a brilliant white light flashed before my eyes, began to surround me, and soon completely engulfed me. The pastor, the choir, the congregation, and the sanctuary disappeared, leaving me alone, kneeling at the base of a heavy wooden post driven deeply into the ground. I was no longer wearing the dress I had worn in church, but instead a heavily textured material covered my body and head. Filled with a deeper sorrow than I had ever felt, I began to weep uncontrollably.

I looked upward and saw a man hanging from the wooden post, which I now realized was not a post but a thick, roughly hewn cross. I watched as blood trickled down his forehead and out of open wounds in his torso, his hands and feet nailed to the cross. The sadness in his face broke my heart as I looked adoringly into his eyes. Despite his agonizing suffering, the man gazed at me with forgiveness and understanding. Feeling unconditional love fill my being, I knew I was looking into the eyes of Jesus Christ.

That evening I rededicated my life to Christ, realizing that my fear of God's abandonment in Shreveport had been a figment of my imagination and immaturity. Now, at age sixteen, I truly knew, without a shadow of a doubt, that God loved me, with no reservation. He had taken me out of my body and transported me to the scene of the Crucifixion in the presence of Jesus Christ.

Not only had my faith in God been restored that evening but I had been honored with a metaphysical spiritual experience directly connected to Christianity. This revival event gave me renewed hope and assurance that the two aspects of my religious life—Christianity and metaphysical spirituality—were sanctioned by God and not incompatible. This new reassurance would be a solid foundation for my future spiritual development.

CHAPTER 5

Comprehending the Therapeutic Functions of Metaphysical Spirituality

Until young adulthood, my knowledge of the therapeutic functions of metaphysical spirituality was limited to out-of-body travel. At the time of each occurrence, the relief from stress allowed me to carry on somewhat normally. Religious instructors, Bible verses, and Baptist sermons had taught me to ask God for healing of both physical and emotional ailments, but, though I did as instructed, demons resulting from my numerous traumatic childhood experiences continued to haunt me, allowing me little peace except during times of out-of-body travel. My religious teachings weren't enough to ease the emotional pain I constantly experienced due to the abuse and my lack of self-worth.

Then, during my first year at Tyler Junior College (TJC), a horrific incident occurred that led to another experience with the therapeutic value of metaphysical spirituality. Immediately after my first semester began, my exuberance at fulfilling a dream of becoming a member of the Apache Belles—the TJC precision drill team—was cut short by a phone call in the middle of the night from my cousin.

"Roy didn't make it, Charlotte," he said, referring to a boy I had dated my junior and senior years of high school in Fort Worth—after which his parents had sent him to Texas Tech University in Lubbock, while my parents had sent me to Tyler Junior College, 443 miles away.

Jolted out of a sleepy daze, I replied, "I don't understand. The doctor released him from the hospital."

"I'll pick you up at your dorm at eight in the morning. I told your parents I would drive you home to Dallas," my cousin added, consolingly.

Since we had started attending different colleges, without my permission Roy had shown up randomly at my college dorm, where he would wait for me to return after dates. Then one night he had called saying he needed to see me the following weekend. I told him I had been invited to a party in Denton, Texas, on Saturday night and would not be available. But he insisted on driving to Denton and meeting me on Sunday morning for breakfast, to which I reluctantly agreed.

On Sunday I borrowed a friend's car and drove to the designated parking lot for our meeting. We spent the morning sitting in Roy's car, as I listened for hours to the many reasons he gave for us to marry. I told him over and over—sweetly and compassionately—I didn't want to get married. I said I felt God had a plan for me in the world, but Roy refused to listen, claiming he couldn't live without me. Exasperated, I suggested we take a break from our discussion and go to a local restaurant for a late breakfast.

When we finished eating, Roy excused himself to go to the bathroom. Several minutes passed before I heard him rapidly approaching me from behind. He lay money on the table and told me to pay the check then meet him at the car. His behavior seemed unusual, and he spoke with a broken voice, which concerned me a little, though I knew he was upset.

When I got to his car, I sat in the front seat ready for another round of disagreements. But instead of arguing Roy informed me that he had swallowed poison in the bathroom. He threw a piece of paper in my lap that read: "Antidote for Mercuric Oxide Poisoning."

"Roy, did you take this?" I demanded. Then he got out of the car and began vomiting. I ran to his side, but by the time I reached him he had collapsed on the wet pavement, his body convulsing. Frantically, I looked for someone to help us. I saw friends arriving at the restaurant and yelled to them to drive Roy to the Denton hospital. They helped me get him into the back seat of their car, and I followed them in Roy's car.

After hours of pumping Roy's stomach and observing him, the doctor on call released him to the care of his parents, who had hurriedly driven to Denton from Fort Worth. I said good-bye, and a friend drove me back to Tyler.

Not until the midnight call from my cousin did I learn that Roy had died in his parents' car on the way home to Fort Worth from the hospital. The poison had burned his mouth, throat, and esophagus, blocking all airflow to his brain. Had he lived, the emergency room doctor at the Fort Worth hospital had told his parents, he would have been a vegetable for the rest of his life.

The next day my cousin drove me home to Dallas, and two days later my parents and I went to Fort Worth for Roy's funeral. At the church, we were seated close to Roy's family. Although I had been raised as a Southern Baptist and was familiar with this church's ritual of open-casket funerals, I had always found it bizarre that people paraded past caskets to view dead bodies. Yet when the sermon ended I had no choice but to join the procession to Roy's casket, dreading what I was about to see.

However, when I looked down at Roy's face, an unusual calmness came over me. I placed my hand on his chest, leaned over the side of the casket, and whispered in his ear, "Roy, I'm so sorry. I'll see you again someday, okay?" As a Christian, I believed in life after death, as well as the teaching that when we die and go to heaven we are reunited with our loved ones.

Customary funeral etiquette dictated that my parents and I go to Roy's house after the burial. At the hospital in Denton, his parents, especially his mother, had made it clear that they blamed me for his death, and I felt anxious. Seconds after we entered the house, I saw his mother making her way toward me through a throng of people. Frightened by the thought of a humiliating confrontation, I froze. But she wrapped her arms tightly around me and whispered in my ear, "Charlotte, don't worry. I don't blame you for Roy's death anymore. Please come with me."

She led me to Roy's bedroom, where he and I had spent many hours listening to our favorite music and watching our favorite movies. She took a piece of paper out of a desk drawer and said, "Read this. It's for you." It was a suicide letter Roy had left me explaining the reason for his intended action and telling me not to blame myself for his shortcomings. I cried as I read this last communication.

"You see, it wasn't your fault," said Roy's mother. "I loved my son dearly, but I know now he was mentally in turmoil, a sick, insecure young man. Please forgive me for the awful things I've said to you." We cried as we held each other. I felt somewhat comforted knowing that they no longer held me responsible for the death of their son.

After my parents and I returned to Dallas, my father initiated a conversation about Roy's death. "You know you're the reason Roy killed himself," he said accusingly. "You played with his emotions. I hope this has taught you not to abuse or disregard the feelings of men who love you."

At my father's accusation that I had been responsible for Roy's death, pain filled my being. I begged repeatedly for God's forgiveness, but the agony of self-blame persisted, and my father's inflammatory words affected every subsequent relationship in which I became involved.

In the spring of 1965, I took my car to a Chevrolet dealership in Dallas for service. Upon returning later to pick it up, I stood behind a crowd and watched through the glass separating the service driveway from the showroom. When I caught sight of my car approaching, I began to weave through the other waiting car owners to get to it. Suddenly, I glimpsed a familiar young man standing twelve to fifteen feet away. His hair was as black as ink; he was dressed in jeans and a short-sleeved white T-shirt; and his piercing dark eyes were fixed on me. My heart beat hard and fast as I pushed through the restless crowd to get to him, certain that the young man was Roy. I was momentarily knocked off balance by another bystander, and when I looked back toward the young man he was no longer there. I scanned every inch of the showroom then walked down the only hallway and looked into each office, but the young man had vanished. After a final search, I concluded that what I had seen was Roy's spirit. I quickly drove away, shaken and wishing I could have talked to him, asked for his forgiveness, and told him I hadn't meant to hurt him.

The appearance of Roy's spirit in the car dealership showroom caused me to again face conflicts between Christianity and metaphysical awareness. My logical side, influenced by religious teachings, told me that I had imagined seeing his spirit, while my metaphysical spiritual side knew it was proof of Christianity's belief in life after death and clear evidence that I was a Christian who also possessed the ability to see spirits. I felt blessed, believing that God had allowed me to experience another aspect of therapeutic metaphysical spirituality. My only regret was that I had been unable to communicate to Roy's spirit the sorrow and guilt I felt about perhaps influencing Roy's decision to commit suicide. I did not feel that in seeing Roy's spirit I had betrayed God and Jesus Christ.

One afternoon years later, after moving to Ruidoso, New Mexico, as I sat on the living room sofa Roy's spirit came to me once again. He wore the same jeans and white T-shirt he had worn at the car dealership in Dallas. The energy of his spirit reflected loving-kindness as he said, "I do not blame you for my death. I was selfish, compulsive, and unthinking of the finality of drinking poison. I only wanted to manipulate you to get my way. I do cherish the time and memories we shared as teenagers. I appeared to you at the car dealership because I wanted you to know I'm happy in the spirit world and to say good-bye—for then."

When he had finished conveying his message, his spirit disappeared. I wept and thanked God for allowing Roy's spirit to visit me and for allowing me the ability to hear his message of forgiveness. His visit solidified my belief in the compatibility of Christianity and metaphysical spirituality and how they could operate in concert. It also comforted me by assuring me of the existence of life after death. As a result, I benefited from a new understanding of an important therapeutic function of metaphysical spirituality—to assist in the release of guilt and shame. I learned that believing in metaphysical spirituality can and does heal the heart. Though sadness and regret about Roy's death remain locked away in a tiny compartment of my heart, the agonizing blame I had originally felt at age eighteen was finally released.

CHAPTER 6

Seeing the Light of God

Regardless of all the contradictions I saw in the Christian religion, I never questioned Christianity's teaching about the existence of life after death. This teaching actually helped me connect the dots between my Christian upbringing and my spiritual gifts. Because I could see the spirits of those who had died, I knew Christianity's teaching about the existence of life after death to be true. But even though I believed in the doctrine I had not yet experienced any part of the spirit world other than seeing the spirits of people who had passed. When I was twenty-one, however, my knowledge of the spirit world expanded greatly.

During a visit to a doctor for infected tonsils, I was told that I needed a tonsillectomy. Prior to the scheduled surgery, I went on a planned deer hunt in south Texas in twenty-degree rainy weather rather than getting the rest recommended by the doctor; and I forgot to take the prescribed antibiotics with me on the trip, making the infection even worse. After returning from the hunt and checking into the hospital, I told the blood technicians, nurses, and orderlies about my negligence and the discomfort I was experiencing.

At 6:00 the following morning, orderlies took me into the operating room, where an anesthesiologist injected medication into the intravenous tube, making me unconscious. Next I remember opening my eyes while lying on the operating table and observing the doctor yank something made of steel out of my mouth, hitting a front tooth hard enough to knock it out. I saw the surgeon pound my chest but I didn't feel it. I saw the nurses stick needles in my shoulders and ankles but still felt no pain.

Then suddenly I felt my body become light and gradually begin to move. Still in a horizontal position, my body rose off the operating table, higher and higher, levitating above it. Then my body assumed a vertical position, before rising even higher. I looked down and saw the operating table, but now it seemed like some other girl lay where I had lain only seconds before.

I heard the doctors and nurses yell with panicked voices as they crammed metal instruments in and out of the girl's mouth and pounded on her chest with their fists like they had done on mine. Then the surgeon grabbed instruments that looked like flat metal paddles, held them over the girl, and yelled, "Clear!" Tremendous jolts of electricity caused the girl's body to jerk violently. The surgeon pounded her chest again, then placed his mouth over her mouth, and repeatedly put the paddles on the girl's chest, although it appeared nothing produced a desired response.

Then the room became brighter white and hazy. The ceiling disappeared, and I floated higher and higher above the operating table as the doctors and the girl on the table below me became smaller and smaller. As they were about to disappear, the continual ascent of my body stalled momentarily. Then my body slowly floated back downward into the hazy white light, though it did not travel toward the operating table but instead approached an empty gurney on the other side of the operating room. My body descended even lower, moved into a horizontal position, and gently landed on the table. I turned my head to the right to observe the medical team as they hovered feverishly over the girl, seemingly too busy with her to notice me. I lay there watching the scene for what seemed a long time before falling asleep.

When I awoke, doctors and nurses stood over me taking blood from my wrist, testing my reflexes, and determining the amount of oxygen in my bloodstream. I remained in the ICU for a couple days then in a private room for a week before being released from the hospital. For weeks afterward, I suffered pains in the joints and muscles where I had seen the nurses stick long needles. When I was physically and emotionally strong enough to question the circumstances of my surgery, my mother told me I had experienced a cardiac arrest and had had no vital signs for four minutes. The doctor had performed CPR—cardiopulmonary resuscitation—using shock paddles and needles. She said the doctor had feared the lack of oxygen to my brain for that length of time might cause permanent damage, leaving me paralyzed or in a vegetative state.

While this part of my experience made sense to me, my mother didn't explain the bright white light I had seen or my flotation above the operating table. I thought perhaps I had been dreaming, but if my experience had been a dream how would I have already known about the shock paddles, the chest beating, and the needles, I wondered. Because my mother seemed distraught talking about my event, I decided not to add to her stress by questioning her further. Yet I knew in my heart that I had experienced something special and unexplainable.

Months after the surgery, my mother and I watched a documentary on television about a phenomenon called near-death experience. As I listened to the details of events described by individuals familiar with this phenomenon—seeing a bright white light, floating upward, entering tunnels, and even encountering dead loved ones—I realized they were describing what had happened to me during my tonsillectomy. They all agreed that they had seen the bright white light of heaven. At that moment, I realized I, too, had seen the light of God. All the people who had reported living through near-death experiences, regardless of their faith, testified to this feeling that they had gone to heaven. Some said deceased loved ones had reached out to help them cross over to the other side. I saw no people during my near-death experience, but it gave me a profound sense of the love and peace associated with death and going to heaven.

Later I had the opportunity to further investigate my near-death experience as I pursued spiritual studies in Ruidoso, New Mexico. Due to information I received from my spiritual teachers, I came to believe that during my near-death experience God had never intended me to become a permanent resident of his kingdom, that his primary purpose in allowing me a glimpse of the other side had been to assure me that the spiritual realm existed. Another purpose had been to expand my knowledge of the spiritual realm. I also realized that he had wanted me to have personal knowledge that religious beliefs and metaphysical beliefs go hand in hand, in this case Christianity's teaching about life after death and the metaphysical experience of going out of body—illustrating another of the many different methods he utilizes to teach us we can integrate religion with our metaphysical beliefs and gifts.

CHAPTER 7

Discovering My Life's Purpose

I recall numerous sermons in church dealing with God having a special purpose for each of us, with the pastors claiming that God would reveal our purposes. This caused me great frustration, because in my twenties I still didn't know my life's purpose. I prayed for God to show me my path clearly and guide me toward it. I knew I possessed some metaphysical abilities—seeing spirits and having out-of-body experiences—but since Christianity didn't embrace such gifts I didn't regard them as indications of my purpose. I thought if I married, gave birth to beautiful children, did volunteer work, and excelled in my real estate career, maybe God would be pleased. Nevertheless, I still experienced a great chasm between my daily life and my inner spiritual longing, both consciously and subconsciously.

Ultimately, it was a shift in geographic location that led me to discover my life's purpose. In 1997, my husband, Don Goodwin, and I were living and working in Colorado when Don began voicing a desire to purchase a retirement home and suggested we travel to the mountainous town of Ruidoso, New Mexico, to view some ten-acre lots advertised in a magazine. I agreed, and one weekend we made the eight-hour road trip.

As we drove down the main street of Ruidoso, I mentioned to Don that the town reminded me of towns in Colorado, with its main street flanked on both sides by tall mountains, something we loved. Further, the town looked quaint and projected some sort of spiritual energy, making us both feel good. By the time we left the area two days later, we had purchased the property we had viewed in a Ranches of Sonterra subdivision.

After returning home, Don encouraged me to quit my job in Colorado and move immediately to Ruidoso to oversee the building of our house, saying he would commute back and forth until he retired. The manager of Ranches of Sonterra had offered me a job selling land in the 3,500-acre subdivision where our property was located. It sounded like fun, but the thought of seeing my husband only on weekends and holidays for two years made me uneasy.

Before making such a crucial decision, I felt I needed to consult others. When I mentioned this to Don's younger sister, she said, "I can't advise you, but I know a psychic you can consult. Her name is Susan Barber."

This concerned me because consulting a psychic

contradicted what my father had taught me. My father had always told me people who went to fortune tellers, or psychics, for advice about life events would go to hell—an idea that scared me. He had told me that no ordinary person could see and hear spirits, saying, "Only God and Jesus Christ, or maybe a special preacher, have those abilities." I still wondered how he could have had a visitation from Christ, and if he was perhaps one of those special people. Still, my need to know if moving to Ruidoso alone was a good option superseded the fear I had about seeing the psychic. I prayed that God wouldn't mind my seeking advice, considering the circumstances.

Before traveling to Dallas and calling the psychic for an appointment, I reflected on the events leading up to the decision to see her. First, my intuition had prompted me to show Don the magazine advertisement about the property in Ruidoso; then the minute we had arrived there he and I had both felt that the town projected spiritual energy; and, lastly, after visiting the property, we had both agreed that it felt right to purchase it.

The following week I flew to Dallas and, after arriving at my mother's house, called the psychic for an appointment, perhaps secretly hoping she would have no time, thus relieving me of any guilt for seeing her. But when I phoned her, she said, "That's wonderful. I just had a cancellation. It's the only opening in my schedule for weeks."

When I arrived at her apartment building, I sat in the car for several minutes, listening to my father's words of warning in my mind. Then I took a deep breath, climbed the stairs, and knocked on her door, hoping I had not made a big mistake.

"Hi there. Come on in," she said, with an inviting smile that spread across a fair, unadorned face framed by dark hair cut in a style reminiscent of Buster Brown's. Relaxed clothing concealed any waistline, and she wore no jewelry.

"I appreciate your seeing me on such short notice," I said. Her friendly demeanor eased my tension somewhat. With a wave of her hand, she motioned me to sit on the sofa across from her. After a minute of conversation, she pressed the record button of a tape recorder on the coffee table and began speaking: "Today is March 31, 1997, and I'm checking to see how many spirit guides you have. I have four. You have three men and two women, so you've got five. They surround you with sound, but you don't always hear them. You're very caught up with your life. You know, we do that. But the more silence you put between you and noise, the better you'll be able to hear them—and possibly see them. You're psychic, too. You know that, don't you? You just don't delve into it the way I do."

I had no idea what Susan meant by spirit guides, and I didn't know if such a concept was compatible with Christianity. I certainly didn't think I was psychic, despite knowing I had some metaphysical gifts.

"You can develop your psychic ability," she said, smiling. "All you have to do is know your spirit guides."

"When we get through with this, I want to tell you some of the experiences I've had, and see what you think," I replied. I thought maybe she would understand the reasons for my many unusual experiences and could offer explanations.

"I'll tell you what, your guides already do talk to you. Many of the thoughts you perceive as yours are really theirs," she continued. "The guides say that they help influence your thoughts, dreams, and directions, but they also let you see where your own self-will lies. Your guides say to just listen to them and they will help you muddle through things, because you are going to see some big changes."

I didn't have a clue what she meant. I decided to share the information about possibly moving to Ruidoso since guidance on that issue had been my sole purpose in contacting a psychic. So I said, "We just bought ten acres in Ruidoso, New Mexico. I am considering moving to Ruidoso to oversee the construction of our retirement house. And I've been offered a job in Ruidoso. I'm trying to decide whether or not to move there now. I need help with that decision."

"I was wondering, because I see you moving your home to Ruidoso. The job you have right now seems to be good for you some of the time, but it doesn't always hold your interest. It's boring you, draining you," she replied.

She was right about my current job. I was bored and fed up working long hours with too few days off.

"You're too spiritually acclimated now for future events, and your soul knows it. The guides say that what you've been offered puts you in the realm of happiness. You're going to love your place. I see you being very happy where you're going. Are you expecting some fame that will come to you from a gift or skill? Are you trying to work on a book?" she said.

"I've always wanted to write a book. I've envisioned myself doing that for years, but I don't know what you mean by fame," I answered, wondering how she knew about my desire to one day write a book.

She continued, "Down the road I see many people coming to meet with you. You're going to be writing and using your gifts. You'd make a great psychic by the way. You have more than one interest in psychic phenomena. You'd like to be able to see visions channeled. Does that intrigue you? There are going to be many people coming to hear what you have to tell them."

At the time, the idea of using the spiritual gifts God had given me to advise other people seemed preposterous, especially since I had a hard time figuring out how to deal with obstacles in my own life, knowing that if I told certain members of my family I was psychic they would think I was going to hell.

Susan continued giving me advice, saying, "Practice channeling. Shut your eyes and ask the guides to come through. Start talking and you'll see they will start talking through you, and you'll know you're not thinking what's coming out. They will show you how they do it."

I didn't understand what she meant by channeling, as I'd never heard of the process.

She then said, "The guides say that you will see visions and know your guides like family, the way I do.

They do want you to spend more time alone anyway, in meditation, because you are going to be a spiritual healer who walks and talks in many places to help others ascend to their spiritual awareness and connectedness."

My head reeled at the thought of becoming a spiritual healer, a term I figured had to have been created by the New Age groups I'd occasionally read about in magazines. Whatever it was, I was certain it had nothing to do with Christianity.

Susan continued, "You're going to be facing four or five years of changes that are quite astounding. It's going to make you more excited about your connection with God. You're going to be needing new shoes once you get to New Mexico, because you're going to be doing a lot of walking. Just know that your guides are going to make your heavenly life on earth more heavenly—by putting you in a great beautiful mountainside to play."

This seemed likely as the job I had been offered involved selling land rather than houses. I was caught off guard at her use of the word God, which was not one I would have expected a psychic to use, though it made me feel more comfortable about having requested Susan's services.

Susan continued with more predictions and even channeled one of her guides, who delivered messages through her. When she finished, she turned off the tape recorder and looked at me with a smile that warmed my heart.

Feeling overwhelmed and tearful, for a moment I couldn't speak, wondering if everything Susan had told me could be true. I knew what I had witnessed, and I wanted desperately to believe her statements, but I was also frightened and skeptical about why God would choose someone as unworthy as myself to be his tool to help others.

Susan then told me she also was a Christian and the daughter of a Baptist preacher. We talked of the religious contradictions she had experienced, and how she understood my dilemma of being a Christian and having metaphysical gifts. She also explained the meanings of spirit guides, out-of-body experiences, and channeling.

Before I left, she gave me more guidance and encouragement, saying, "You can do this. It is your life now. Listen to your innermost thoughts in your head and know your guides are speaking with you. Sit quietly with paper and pen, and wait. Your guides, in their own time, will begin moving the pen and your hand. It's called automatic writing and will begin the communication with your guides. But you will have to be patient, for everything is in God's time, not yours."

I felt relief at her understanding of my dilemma and excitement about what my future might hold. I still couldn't fathom what my new life might encompass, but I knew in my heart I had to find out. Susan had convinced me that I, too, was psychic—giving me self-confidence about my metaphysical abilities—and, as a result, had a lifetime of wondrous things to experience and do. Her predictions suggested my life's purpose of helping and healing others through use of my metaphysical spiritual gifts and that Ruidoso was the place where I was to develop my spiritual gifts and begin writing my first book. By the time I left her apartment, I had made the decision to move to Ruidoso as soon as possible, but for a much greater reason than overseeing the building of our retirement house and selling vacant land.

The next day, I flew home to Colorado and shared my experience with Don. Despite my astonishment, he wrapped his arms around me and told me he supported me on whatever path I chose to follow. I immediately resigned my job and moved to Ruidoso, alone, to oversee the building of our new house and begin the new life Susan's guides had predicted.

Once settled in a rented duplex, when I wasn't selling land in Ranches of Sonterra I practiced automatic writing as Susan had instructed. Around the time exasperation was about to get the best of me, Spirit moved my hand, and the pen scribbled words and pictures on the paper. The first spirit to communicate said his name was Job from the Bible. Initially, I was dubious that a spirit had really moved my hand, but I chose to believe it anyway, which filled my heart with joy.

From that day forward, my automatic writing became increasingly clearer, eventually occurring in complete sentences. I also glimpsed a spirit or two in my duplex. Soon I resigned my sales job to have even more time to develop my psychic skills.

Later, in researching the terms "spiritual" and "spirituality," I came across the following explanations that expanded my understanding. Philip D. Kenneson wrote in his article "What's in a Name? A Brief Introduction to the Spiritual but Not Religious": "Religious conveys an institutional connotation, usually associated with Abrahamic traditions: to attend worship services, to say Mass, to light Hanukkah candles. To be spiritual, in contrast, connotes personal practice and personal empowerment having to do with the deepest motivations of life."[1] Further, in his book *After the Baby Boomers: How Twenty- and Thirty-Somethings Are Shaping the Future of American Religion*, Robert Wuthnow wrote: "Spirituality is about much more than going to church and agreeing or disagreeing with church doctrines. Spirituality is the shorthand term used in Western society to talk about a person's relationship with God."[2]

With my move to Ruidoso, my true spiritual journey began. I came to understand the meaning of embracing both Christianity and metaphysical spirituality. Also, my purpose in life was finally revealed: I felt that God had given me the information and gifts required to help others who had conflicts between religious beliefs and metaphysical gifts similar to those with which I had struggled.

CHAPTER 8

Developing Spiritual Gifts and Controlling Personal Environments

During my time living in Ruidoso, I continued developing my spiritual gifts and learning how to control my environments. About a year after my move there, our new house was finished and I devoted even more time to developing my gifts of communication with Spirit. Occasionally, I questioned if my actions were right or wrong in the eyes of God, asking how something that felt so heavenly could be wrong and each time receiving reassurance that it was not. The unconditional love I sensed when a spiritual being visited me reinforced my belief that Christianity and metaphysical spirituality were compatible. Finally, I ceased questioning and simply had faith that God would not allow me to go down a false path.

I performed automatic writing whenever I felt the urge from spirit, sitting for hours in the hopes that I would receive messages from the spiritual realm. Susan had told me that everything occurred in God's time, so I tried to be patient. Every day I asked Spirit to make me aware of its presence by touching my hair or skin, or giving me another sign. Yearning for confirmation of their presence other than through automatic writing, I also asked spirits to take me traveling with them at night.

One day while walking across my living room, I heard someone speaking. The voice sounded like mine, but the words and phrases didn't. At that moment, I realized for the first time that the voices I had often heard in my head were actually the voices of my spirit guides and that my concern for betraying my religion plus my own thoughts of limitation had kept me from hearing them earlier in my life. Exuberant about this breakthrough, I celebrated my achievement.

Now I rejoiced in my spirit guides' words of love and support of my endeavors to become ever closer to God and Christ. My spirit guides shared their knowledge of the spirit world and gave me instructions on how to proceed with my spiritual journey. They explained why I had had such horrific experiences in life, telling me that God's desire for me to teach others how to heal required experiencing hardships myself. They taught me that we are living in a classroom where every incident and relationship—good or bad—offers a lesson. They further revealed that everything unfolding is a part of God's master plan, the process by which God teaches us how we grow in awareness and follow a more spiritual path. My spirit guides further taught me not to fear my metaphysical abilities but to accept them as gifts from God for the benefit of myself and humankind.

I also began to experience out-of-body travel with my spirit guides and knew it was, indeed, what I had done as a child to escape my parents' abusive fighting. Not only did my spirit guides visit me regularly but so did other spirits whom I could both see and hear, including those of my father, my husband's father and grandparents, my deceased aunts and uncles, and friends. My spirit guides taught me to channel, as I had seen Susan do, and told me to channel their messages to friends and clients. By now I had clients who paid me fees for spiritual guidance, readings, or contacting loved ones who had crossed over in death.

At the beginning of my spiritual journey in Ruidoso, before I had been given any instruction from a living person, I had not known there were different kinds of spirits that presented themselves to people who were open to them. Now I could discern different spirits from their various tones—the sweet ones, the jokesters, and the angry ones. However, I had yet to learn the art of negotiating with them to control my environment. Most nights after going to bed I didn't sleep because the prevailing energy I felt in my bedroom frightened me, keeping me awake until the first light of day.

A few months after I'd moved into my newly built house, a friend introduced me to Jean Stanfield, an ordained metaphysical minister. I was inspired by her knowledge of the metaphysical world and her healing abilities, and she soon became my spiritual mentor. Every day she taught me the ways of spirit guides—seeing them, hearing them, feeling them, and channeling them. My spirit guides also gave me instruction, but having a living individual with whom I could talk gave me a different level of comfort. I told her about a number of the scary voices and activities I had seen and heard at night in my house, and she taught me that not all spirits are created equal. She gave me protection prayers to recite, and taught me how to stand in my own power so I could control the energy in my environment. For example, to dispel negative energy from a setting I was to say the following:

> *We speak to all misqualified energy: You have no power. Your day is done. In God's name, I AM. Be thou dissolved into light, illumination, and love forever.*

> I was encouraged to add when necessary:

> *I command you to leave my house and my presence, and not come back. According to the Spiritual Law of the Universe, you must do as I say.*

> By contrast, to attract positive energy to a setting I was to say the following:

> *I welcome spirits of the Christ Light to be present.*

I welcome my spirit guides of the Christ Light to be present.

As a result of saying these prayers, I gradually learned how to dismiss the angry, lesser-evolved, misguided spirits from my house and encourage the loving, sweet spirits of the Christ Light to surround me. The protection prayers ultimately gave me confidence that I have some control over my environment.

This mentor also inspired me to expand my spiritual knowledge by learning different means of energy healing. A gifted healer, she taught me Reiki—a form of energy healing reflecting the golden elemental earth healing energy—and eventually I became a Reiki master. With a woman in Sedona, Arizona, I studied Seichem, a form of energy healing that incorporates the energy of fire, water, and earth—and became a Seichem master. Spirit, as well as other practitioners, told me that these two healing modalities could further enhance my spiritual journey and my knowledge of the spirit world. The lessons I learned in energy healing led to my becoming a vessel for Spirit to heal others through hands-on healing. I became a certified metaphysical practitioner in order to professionally engage in the treatment of physical and mental ailments and conditions through the use of Spiritual Mind Treatment. Later, through correspondence courses I also became an ordained Metaphysical Minister.

The increased acceleration and intensity of my spiritual journey upon arriving in Ruidoso seemed to be no accident. I believe God wanted me in Ruidoso—alone—to truly know him outside of what I had been taught in church. I believe Spirit led me to the session with psychic Susan in 1997, and as a result, I chose to change my life and focus more on metaphysical spirituality.

Ultimately, I became a spiritual healer exactly as Susan and her spirit guides had envisioned during my visit. Because of the teachings of Christ, my spirit guides, and other master teachers who graced me with their presence in Ruidoso, the idea of betraying God by having metaphysical gifts and beliefs became for me a notion only taught by organized religion, and all guilt associated with that notion disappeared.

I lived in Ruidoso for most of five years, and Don never retired. I missed Don tremendously, but I never felt lonely. I came to know a houseful of loving, sometimes playful spirits who kept me company. Then for two years Don and I lived in Orange County, California, where he took a vice chancellorship position with a large community college district, after which I returned to Ruidoso and stayed until I felt my time there was over.

As a result of all I learned about the spirit world in Ruidoso, I have integrated my Christian beliefs with my metaphysical spiritual practices as I teach and heal others. When working with others, I am careful to explain that my gifts come from God, as I want them to understand that I am nothing without the guidance of God and Spirit. Whether people possess spiritual gifts or not, I desire that they not fear the spirit world, as spirits are with us at all times.

Most spirits with whom I've been in contact during my lifetime have had positive energy. The presence of these heavenly spirits can sometimes bring us to tears because of the unconditional love they project. Their desire is to help with our daily problems, and they only want the best for us.

By contrast, spirits who have not moved into the Light of Christ and have negative energy need a little nudge in the right direction. The reasons spirits do not move into the Light of Christ are varied: they died in a manner not comforting to their souls; they had no relatives or loved ones to help them cross over; they're angry or don't understand why they left the physical plane so rapidly; or they loved their physical existence on earth and are not yet ready to move into the Light of Christ. The few times I have experienced spirits with negative energy I've said protection prayers and demanded the spirits move into the Light of Christ, seeing them comply. Any time we experience negative energy in our surroundings we need to stand in our own power and tell the spirits they must move on. The energy from these spirits can be frightening, but it is our responsibility to aid them by moving them into the light of the spiritual plane. The protection prayers I learned have not only helped me move a few misguided spirits into the Light of Christ but also allowed me peaceful sleep at night.

Since we do not live in a perfect world and sometimes there is conflict between people, another prayer I have found helpful, taking a deep breath before saying it, is the following:

> *My sweet spirit guides, please fill my head and send out of my mouth only the words you want me to hear and say. Help me stay calm and not blurt out hurtful and tactless words that can't be taken back.*

In addition to the use of protection prayers to help control my environment, I have found that paying attention to the messages of spirit guides and angels God sends us can help me make better choices. I also have made better decisions while listening to voices in my head and paying attention to any uncomfortable feelings in my gut. I have found that when I ignore the voices and my innermost feelings I make my biggest mistakes. Although listening to voices in the head has been described by many as a symptom of delusion, it is my belief that embracing the abilities God gave us when we were put on this earthly plane, including listening to our inner voices, leads to enhancement of our lives.

CHAPTER 9

Spiritual Loss and Disconnection

As time passed, I felt comfortable in my growth as a spiritual healer and continued to integrate my Christian and metaphysical beliefs. After I had returned to Ruidoso from California, Don moved to Albuquerque, New Mexico, for another college administration position. Since commuting from different cities was taking a toll on our time together, in 2003 we sold our house in Ruidoso and I relocated to Albuquerque, where I spent time writing my first book, *The Twisted Path*. Then in 2006 we moved to Pagosa Springs, Colorado, where we felt more at home. After a year of retirement, Don became bored and resumed working in his beloved field of education, while I completed my book, which was published in 2008.

As I became established in Pagosa Springs and the public became aware of my book and my spiritual gifts, I began receiving calls and emails requesting my services of energy healing and channeling, as well as requests from online magazines for spiritual articles. Not until email requests for spiritual counseling and readings arrived from people across the United States and overseas did I understand the far reach of the Internet, and working with clients in this way was a method I grew to enjoy. My integrated belief system was an aid in helping others. The Christian aspect of my work gave people a sense of peace and dispelled the idea that they were engaging in a New Age activity, while the metaphysical aspect of my work intrigued those not very familiar with the spiritual realm.

I felt self-confident sharing the messages of the beautiful, sweet spirits who surrounded me daily and performing the services I offered. I had no reservations about any of these activities until one afternoon when the wife of a favorite cousin who lived in Southern California phoned me and said, "Charlotte, I need your help. Jimmy has suffered a massive heart attack and is in the hospital. I just found out he has incurable cancer he didn't tell me about. I'm so worried. Will you please check with Spirit and see if he is okay?"

It had never been my practice to tell someone the details of their death or a loved one's death, regardless of whether I could see them or not. I knew that the ebb and flow of life and death came in God's time, not ours, and I didn't want to misconstrue the meaning of any message concerning a death. But Spirit gave me a message for my cousin's wife, and I replied, "I'm so sorry for Jimmy. Please know that Jimmy chose not to tell you because he loves you more than anything and didn't want to scare you when he didn't know how long he had to live. He now realizes it wasn't the correct way to handle the information he received from his doctors, and he is sorry. Life and death is in God's time, and Jimmy and God will make the determination as to when Jimmy will leave us."

As I listened to her weep and beg for more information, I agreed I would speak to Spirit and call her back momentarily. I hung up and began praying, asking Spirit to help me answer her question. Words began flowing inside my mind. When it was clear Spirit was finished, I called my cousin's wife and reported, "Spirit told me Jimmy is okay. I see him smiling and sitting in a chair." I told her of the vision Spirit had shared about Jimmy's current condition. She seemed relieved.

Two days later Jimmy's wife called again and said as she wept, "The day after I spoke to you the nurses helped Jimmy out of bed, and he sat in a chair like you said. For two days he seemed better, but then he took a turn for the worse and died, Charlotte. Why did he die? You told me Spirit said he was okay. Why did you tell me that when it wasn't true?"

I apologized, and wept myself, as I loved Jimmy and I was going to miss his positive outlook on life and the wonderful music he played on his guitar. I begged his wife to forgive me.

Her question of why I had told her something untrue undermined my self-confidence. I didn't understand why Spirit had given me such a message either. I thought perhaps I had misconstrued the message. Upset, thinking I had given her incorrect information, for several days I asked Spirit, "Why?" Then I received the answer: "When Jimmy's wife asked if he would be okay, we answered her question correctly since at that time—two days before his death—Jimmy was, indeed, okay. We told you he would sit in a chair and smile. On the third day, his soul decided his time on earth had come to an end. Jimmy decided he didn't want his wife to deal with the agony of the cancer that raged inside his body. It was Jimmy who chose to leave." The explanation Spirit gave me let me know I had heard Spirit correctly. Nonetheless, my heart ached for perhaps causing additional pain to my cousin's wife.

Subsequently, I continued to work with clients but less and less often, turning down requests for appointments. I began questioning if God really wanted me to continue spiritual healing and concluded that I should take a break from such work. Unwittingly, I began to cease daily interaction with my spirit guides, making the excuse that I didn't have time.

Meanwhile, Don decided to finally retire and wanted to travel, so we leased a house in San Miguel de Allende, Mexico, for six months. I thought getting away from my usual routines would allow me to start writing another book. As soon as we made the decision, a man from out of town offered us cash for our house, stipulating that he could acquire it in three weeks. Ultimately, instead of spending six months in Mexico we decided to move to a gated community in East Texas so we could be close to family and childhood friends.

Having grown up in East Texas as the daughter of a Baptist minister, I already knew this was one of the most conservative religious parts of the country and that the residents would not understand how my ability to see and hear spirits could be compatible with my Christian belief in God and Jesus Christ. The probability of that attitude having a negative impact on our new living arrangements worried me, but I thought perhaps I could make it work by taking a break from my spiritual pursuits and by keeping a low profile.

Consequently, I bought back inventoried copies of my book from Amazon and my distributor and decided not to disclose my spiritual gifts to anyone in this very religious and spiritually close-minded community. Nor did Don and I join a church here, both feeling that church wasn't a brick-and-mortar building to go to in order to be close to God. When friends and acquaintances asked why we hadn't joined a church, we answered, "We're still looking," a remark that seemed to satisfy them.

Despite my adjustments, living in our East Texas community became more and more uncomfortable on a spiritual level. The happiness I thought I would find being close to relatives only existed when we were with them. And although Don and I made wonderful friends, as the years passed I felt nothing but loneliness in a room full of people. I also felt increasingly disconnected from the spirit guides who had supported me through their unconditional love.

One day I began crying out loud and said, "Donnie, I want to go home," knowing for certain that my soul yearned for the spiritual connection I had given up when we had moved from Pagosa Springs.

My disconnection from my spirit guides had led to a feeling of undeniable loss. Over the five and a half years of living in East Texas, my recognition of the person looking back every time I gazed in a mirror had dwindled so much that eventually I could see and feel my spiritual self, my true self, totally vanishing.

I knew that I alone had been the cause of my spiritual regression: I had shut out the spirits who had taught me I could integrate my Christian beliefs with my practices as a metaphysical spiritual healer. As a result, the spiritual energy that had once flowed so freely seemed blocked, and I could no longer see and hear spirits clearly. Once in a while, when sitting in my bedroom at night watching television, I thought I glimpsed a spirit standing in the doorway, but as soon as I turned my head to see more clearly, the image disappeared. Not only did my soul hunger for the metaphysical spiritual activity I had given up when moving to East Texas, but I wanted to write again and felt I needed the Southwest as my inspiration. So we sold our house in Texas and bought one in Santa Fe, New Mexico.

Three weeks before our move to Santa Fe, the editor of a community magazine called to say she had read my book, *The Twisted Path*, and wanted an interview before I left Texas. I was taken aback, since I had removed the book from distribution channels and confided in only seven people about my gifts. However, after asking Spirit to protect me, I agreed to the interview and proceeded to answer all the editor's questions honestly and truthfully, explaining how metaphysical spirituality reinforced and enhanced my Christian beliefs and my love of God and Jesus Christ.

The community reactions to the interview gave me unexpected encouragement and support. The day the magazine hit the community's mailboxes, my phone began to ring. The first call came at 9:30 p.m. from a ninety-five-year-old woman, who said, "Honey, God is proud of you and your honesty. I know you are a Christian." Another person rang our doorbell at 9:00 p.m. the next night and left a present on the porch. The following week others called and sent emails saying they wanted to read *The Twisted Path*, even those I knew to be strict Christians. In addition, a number of people wanted to meet me before I left for New Mexico, and I made time for all of them. One had been a metaphysical practitioner before moving to East Texas and had feared telling anyone about her gifts. Another woman's deceased husband had stood by her bedside every night after she turned out the lights, but her fear had caused him to disappear. She asked me how to overcome her fear so he might stay and have a conversation. Others reported they had various spiritual gifts but were afraid of anyone finding out, each saying something like, "I just wish I had known you were here. I would have loved to have someone to talk to." They had all suffered in silence, as I had so many years before.

I urged them to continue their spiritual endeavors and embrace their metaphysical experiences assured that this would not detract from their Christianity. I told them of the spiritual loss I had been feeling and advised them not to make the same mistake. I was honored by their responses, feeling the tremendous respect they showed for my spiritual gifts. Only a handful of friends distanced themselves, disapproving of my past metaphysical practices; I understood and chose not to confront them about their actions.

Upon first moving to East Texas and going in the closet regarding my spiritual metaphysical activities, I had had no idea how detrimental that decision would be for my soul. I had walked away from my spirit guides, closing the door between me and the spirit world out of concern about religious ridicule. I had lacked the courage and conviction to stand up for my belief in integrating Christianity and metaphysical spirituality. But after the article came out exposing my gifts to the community, I felt relief and joy to discover that hearing about the conflicts and personal spiritual growth I had experienced could inspire others on their own spiritual quests. As a result, I promised God, Jesus Christ, and my spirit guides that nothing would ever cause me to deny my metaphysical beliefs again, and that I would continue working to help guide and heal others.

A gift for you

Read this and know you are not alone
and there are many others that share
what you have been blesssed with.
Embrace your God given gifts my friend.
From Jim Petitpren

CHAPTER 10

Spiritual Rediscovery

Living in East Texas in no way affected my Christian beliefs, as my love of God and Jesus Christ never wavered. It was only because the religious beliefs of the community differed from mine due to my integration of metaphysical beliefs that I had felt emptiness from my loss of spiritual connection. When we crossed the state line into New Mexico, I anticipated reconnecting with my spirit guides. And I thought that if I moved back to the land where my spiritual gifts originally manifested, they would immediately return in full force.

After moving into our new house, I prayed to God every day and talked to my spirit guides every night. I asked God for protection in our new surroundings and to give us good health, happiness, and prosperity in all aspects of life. I asked my spirit guides for forgiveness for my disconnection from them for six years and to allow me the honor of seeing and hearing them again. For weeks nothing came, but I knew they were listening.

Several friends who were healers, psychics, and mediums aware of my hope to regain connection to the spirit world said, "Charlotte, you've been on a six-year sabbatical. Your gifts will come back. They may be different, but they will come back stronger than before. Quit worrying and just let the spirits do their work."

Even so, to renew my hope I again searched the Bible for verses about having spiritual gifts and found the following, which helped reassure me that my gifts would return:

> "To each is given the manifestation of the Spirit for the common good." (*Revised Standard Version*, 1 Cor. 12.7)

> "To one is given through the Spirit the utterance of wisdom, and to another the utterance of knowledge according to the same Spirit." (1 Cor. 12.8)

> "Having gifts that differ according to the grace given to us, let us use them: if prophecy, in proportion to our faith; if service, in our serving; he who teaches, in his teaching; he who exhorts, in his exhortation; he who contributes, in liberality; he who gives aid, with zeal; he who does acts of mercy, with cheerfulness." (Rom. 2:6–8)

One day as I looked for a movie to watch on television while Don watched football I discovered *Keepers of the Light* directed by Adrian Carr and Pamela Weaver. It was about a woman in California who had experienced a number of disturbing events that prompted her quest for a life of greater purpose, beginning with traveling to Peru to study with a shaman named Puma. Because Don and I had studied with Puma during a spiritual trip to Peru in 1999, I was sure God had made me aware of the movie. During one scene, Puma said, "My grandfather always taught me it's necessary to go to sleep in order to wake up." His words made me suddenly realize that I had been asleep for six years, ignoring why God had put me on this earth, hiding my God-given spiritual gifts, and purposely detaching myself from the spirit world, afraid of religious ridicule in a close-minded society. I further realized that it would take time to renew some of the spirit relationships of the past, as well as make new ones. I knew I had to elevate my vibrational energy from one associated with uninspired nonmetaphysical believers to one in tune with the spirits. I was sure that God had sent me, through the movie, a message of patience. As a result, I relaxed a little while continuing my efforts to reacquaint myself with my spirit guides.

Gradually, I began to experience an increase in spirit activity at night. I heard spirits in our bedroom bumping into furniture, and opening and closing drawers in our bathroom; I saw a man and woman dressed in evening wear—him in a tuxedo and her in a floor-length evening gown—walk hand in hand across the room; I also saw a young person standing by my bed staring at me, as if wanting to talk; I felt a spirit climb into bed and rustle the covers after Don had gotten up in the morning; and I even heard a spirit say my name. I was elated, because all these incidents were similar to ones I had initially experienced during my spiritual journey in Ruidoso.

One important and thrilling visitation occurred in my office while I was writing. I was playing a CD of spiritual music, as was my custom when writing, and had lit a white candle and a stick of incense to enhance my spiritual awareness. I had also said a prayer asking for spirit guides of the Christ Light to fill my mind with the proper words and carry them out of my fingertips to the keyboard of my computer. When the last word of the prayer had passed my lips, three beautiful spirits from my past reunited above my head—Jesus Christ; my protector, Archangel Michael; and my master teacher, Moses—as the ceiling of my office opened up to heaven. The familiar feeling of unconditional love rushed through my body, and I began to weep as I looked at their lovely faces. None of the spirits spoke, but the love they exuded made me certain that God still had a purpose for me using my metaphysical abilities.

Since that day, God has given me additional confirmation that my gifts would return. I have met a gifted spiritual teacher, Adara, a new mentor whom God has placed on my path. Aware of my past abilities, she is helping me gain an even greater understanding of the spirit world than I had before. When I now ask the spirits of the Christ Light to appear, I see, hear, and channel spirits who have been a part of my spiritual path in the past, as well as those new to my spiritual realm, all present to enhance my knowledge and experience. I am excited at the speed with which my gifts are returning and am comforted knowing God is in charge.

When I moved to Santa Fe, I was sure that I would not experience issues about the melding of Christianity and metaphysics because many practitioners of metaphysics live in the area. But in mid-May 2018, I again had to defend my melded beliefs of Christianity and metaphysical spirituality. One evening Don and I invited a good friend and his father, who was visiting him from out of state, for a glass of wine. As we sat on the patio enjoying the beautiful New Mexico weather, the friend—aware of my metaphysical beliefs and memoir—brought up the subject of my spiritual gifts of clairvoyance, clairaudience, and clairsentience. As he spoke, I realized from the expression on his father's face that I should address the issue.

"I am a Christian," I told the man. "I have a love for God and Jesus Christ that transcends all else. But I also have spiritual gifts. I see, I hear, and I feel spirits, and I've performed energy healing and am even an ordained metaphysical minister."

"Well, I think you're a little delusional and unrealistic," the man said, smiling slightly. "How can you call yourself a Christian when you're telling me you can see and hear spirits? I think not."

"Why can't you accept that I can be a Christian and also have metaphysical gifts?" I asked.

Then I shared a bit of my life story with the man, emphasizing how my father had raised me as a Baptist, and told him about a couple of mysterious experiences I'd had, in the hope that I could open his mind to the possible coexistence of these contrasting beliefs.

"God spoke to Moses," I said. "Certainly, I'm not comparing my lowly self to a man of that stature, but it is written in many places throughout the Bible that Christ spoke to his disciples and followers after his resurrection. The Bible also mentions God giving his followers a variety of spiritual gifts. Granted it's 2018, but if it occurred in the time of Christ and beyond why not now, and why not to someone like me?" The man shifted his position and didn't respond. I figured he had no answer.

Finally, his son said, "It's getting late. I think we should call it a night."

Don and I ushered them to the front door, then the man thanked us for the wine and walked out. His son, in an effort to ease any tension, kissed me on the cheek and whispered in my ear, "I'm a believer, Charlotte. I'll talk to you soon."

After this incident, I felt pleased with the growth in my spiritual attitude. In the past, having my Christianity questioned had always caused me pain, and those who did not understand how metaphysical spirituality enhances religion had frustrated me. But because of this experience I now realized that, after the devastation of losing my spiritual connection and the exuberant experience of rediscovering it, my belief in embracing both Christian divinity and metaphysical spirituality was much stronger than any fear I had of skepticism or ridicule.

CHAPTER 11

Learning about the Art of Dying

Witnessing or learning about the dying process can help dispel fears people have of death and reveal greater fundamental truths about religious and spiritual belief systems. Growing up in a religious environment and attending a lot of funerals, I heard preachers talk about deceased people joining family and loved ones in heaven and being with Christ, messages that were intended to underscore the existence of life after death. However, it wasn't until I had concrete experiences with the dying process that I felt a sense of peace concerning death.

That reassuring feeling of peace arose in response to specific knowledge I had received from my own near-death experience. When my near-death experience occurred, I didn't comprehend its significance other than being aware that it went far beyond my knowledge of Christian teachings. I had questions I felt could not be answered by typical Christian explanations, and the idea of metaphysical spirituality was still foreign to me. Not until decades later, following repeated exposures, did I better comprehend its meaning in terms of the actual process of dying.

Most people do not understand near-death experiences or know much about the dying process. Nor do Christian teachings reveal much information about the dying process. However, many people I have spoken to over the years wanted to better understand it. They told me that they feared what happens when people are about to die and wondered if the dying process was painful, if they would hallucinate about seeing deceased relatives, or if they would actually see people, places, and things to which they could relate. I understood their hesitancy to believe in spirit contact, for during my Christian upbringing I had never heard about such things.

When I volunteered in the emergency room at Parkland Hospital in Dallas, I saw people die from illnesses, traffic accidents, and gunshot or knife wounds. Though their deaths were tragic, I remained detached, not yet having awareness of the metaphysical spirit world. My first involvement with a person dying occurred with the passing of my mother three months prior to her one-hundredth birthday. For a couple years before my mother died, she often saw and talked with her deceased mother, father, and sisters. On several occasions, I witnessed her conversing with someone standing at the foot of her bed. Those were happy moments, evidenced by her laughter and smiles. She sometimes expressed a fear of dying, but her fear seemed to ease the more she communicated with the visiting spirits. I felt comforted by my mother's visits from spirits, feeling her conversations with them were with her deceased family and friends who would help her cross over to the spiritual plane when she was ready to go.

I learned more about my mother's experiences from books given to our family members by hospice caregivers, describing events preceding the impending death of loved ones. One such book was *Gone from My Sight: The Dying Experience* by Barbara Karnes, RN, who, in addressing disorientation occurring within two weeks of death, wrote, "A person often becomes confused, talking to people, and about places and events that are unknown to others. They may see and converse with loved ones who have died before them."[1] Other books referred to similar occurrences, one even calling the instances of seeing others "metaphysical experiences."

The morning I realized my mother had only a short time to live she began tilting her head upward and staring into space as if looking at someone. I sat by her bedside all day and into the night, but she no longer spoke to me and had little recognition of her surroundings. That evening she had weak circulation and pulse, her limbs had become cold, and her skin had begun to change color. Although she showed no awareness of my presence, I knew her soul was listening, so I told her repeatedly that she could leave, that my brother and I would be fine, finally saying emphatically, "Mamma, go. You must go now."

At that she slowly moved her head to a position where she could focus on me. Her green eyes now looking black as coal, she gazed directly into my eyes, drew her last breath, and exhaled with a sigh. At the moment my mother looked at me with those black eyes, I knew her soul had departed.

I have been taught many lessons about death by my spirit guides and angels. They have told me that when it is time for us to die Spirit takes our soul from our body before we draw our last breath, explaining that this keeps us from feeling the pain of physical death. I do not believe my mother felt pain when her body began to shut down, since it appeared that she had already withdrawn her awareness from our earthly plane. I believe the only reason she lowered her head and looked at me was to say good-bye and let me know her soul had departed.

My spirit guides have also taught me that our deceased relatives and friends begin to visit us long before our soul departs. They also told me that spirits help the soul's transition into the spirit world, alleviating fear and worry.

When I began my spiritual journey in Ruidoso, I better understood why God had allowed me my own brief encounter with death in a near-death experience. It was to give me personal knowledge of the integration of Christianity and metaphysical spirituality and personal knowledge about what happens to us when we die.

Moreover, I believe God's purpose in allowing me to witness my mother's dying process was twofold as well: to let me know that her constant communication with visiting spirits was proof that they join us prior to death to help us transition to the spirit world and to provide the knowledge that the soul leaves the body before our last breath. As a result of these revelations, I now better understand the dying process and take comfort in the fact that our spirit families help with this transition.

Both Christianity's belief in life after death and metaphysical spirituality's belief that spirits are by our bedside before and during death contribute to my belief that the dying process is an art form orchestrated by God. Further, the dying process can prompt witnessing Christians and others to consider that truth lies in the integration of conflicting belief systems.

CHAPTER 12

Understanding God's Angels and Metaphysical Spirit Guides

During my spiritual journey, I have gradually learned how angels referenced in the Bible and the spirit guides of metaphysical spirituality both demonstrate God's love and are used by God to help people. At the onset of my spiritual journey in 1997, the psychic I went to in Dallas introduced me to the term "spirit guides." When researching the term in the Bible, I found verses about spirits and guidance implying that it was a sin to seek guidance from mediums or psychics and referencing Satan and his demonic spirits. I found no verses about spirit guides, the wonderful spirits who graced me with their presence every day. Hoping to discover more, I researched *The Book of Knowledge: The Keys of Enoch* by J. J. Hurtak, which said, "You are given spiritual Masters and Guides who will take you into other kingdoms, but they are your redeemers only in so far as they work with the Christ . . ."[1] This book reinforced my new belief in spirit guides and my Christian belief that such spirits work with Christ.

As I grew spiritually, I compared other Bible verses to the teachings of my spirit guides and to my personal beliefs to further understand the differences. I found that many books of the Bible spoke of God's angels and their purposes in our lives, such as the following lines:

> "For He will give His angels charge of you, to guard you in all your ways." (*Revised Standard Version* Bible, Ps. 91:11)

> "For it is written, 'He will give His angels charge of you, to guard you.'" (Lk. 4:10)

According to the Bible, angels, defined as supernatural beings who have never lived on the earth plane, are sent to care for us, protect us, and act as messengers of God. It is said that after childhood there is an angel assigned to each person for a lifetime, information that assured me people are protected from harm.

I also learned that the purpose of spirit guides differs from the purpose of angels in particular ways. Spirit guides, who may be deceased relatives or friends, or beings we have never known, teach us the lessons of life, giving us information to help us make decisions; they are our instructors. Spirit guides come when we need them, and when their job is complete they leave, not staying with us all the time like our angel. Similarly, master teachers who lived on this earthly plane as masters in their times but are now in the spirit world, come to impart great knowledge and wisdom.

My communication with spirit guides and master teachers has been frequent, intimate, and inspirational. I received messages from spirit guides and master teachers every day during my spiritual training in Ruidoso, which gave me a feeling of peacefulness and closeness to God. One day I received a letter that challenged the validity of the messages I was receiving from my spirit guides, causing me to temporarily reassess all communications. The letter was from a cousin, a devout Baptist Christian who had heard about my spiritual transformation. Calling into question the validity of my road to enlightenment and my spiritual metaphysical gifts, he said that New Age followers were sinning against God and talked about Satan's influence on those who follow the metaphysical path, telling me I walked with Satan on my new path. Insulted and hurt, I replied, saying, "Not I. I have never walked with Satan. I have only walked with the loving spirits whom God has placed in my path."

The conflict I had earlier experienced between Christianity and metaphysical spirituality surfaced again in my mind. I decided to ask Spirit about it. Previously, I had told Spirit of my concern about religious teachings differing from metaphysical teachings. An instant after asking Spirit to address my concerns I heard a beautiful voice say: "You were a religious child, and growing up in that environment you did not have a chance to see and hear and feel the truth, the light, and the way. As an adult, you have had the ability and the time to analyze what is truly true. You have seen and been told what is truly true.

"Do not feel guilty, but be relieved you have the right as an individual to think and feel however you choose. If you see and feel the images you have been shown, the visions you have been shown, the channeling you have had with the many spirits I have allowed to present themselves to you, then you know the way, the truth, and the light. Do not let anyone tell you anything different from what you have learned on your own.

"I have been with you since the beginning, before you came to earth. You know me and who I am. You are not wrong, and do not feel guilty for knowing what God has taught you, what Spirit has taught you, and what we will continue to teach you. Feel good and feel blessed that you are one who has allowed yourself to be open to our teachings.

"The world and those within it are one. We are one. Believe it, trust it, and know it with all your heart. You will not be led astray by any of us. I am God, the One, the only One, the Almighty, and the One who loves you the most. It's that simple. Go now and worry no more, for I am with you."

I felt in my heart and gut that what the channeled voice had said was true. After that day, regardless of what anyone said to me I no longer doubted that my metaphysical beliefs and gifts agreed with my Christian teachings. I no longer doubted the messages I received from angels and spirit guides, or the images I saw of beings from the spiritual realm.

From my experiences with angels, as well as what I have heard about others' experiences with them, I believe angels present themselves at the most appropriate times. For example, angels appeared to me once to help me to a new path when I needed encouragement and guidance after a horseback riding accident in California, which had me in a wheelchair, using a walker, and on crutches for several months. I had difficulty getting out of bed in the mornings due to the pain, and one morning as I lay in bed on my right side, I heard children giggling and felt a poke in my back. I turned over and saw two precious, chubby-cheeked little angels who looked like cherubs propped up on their elbows on a pillow. One of them said in a childlike voice, "It's time to get out of bed. Today is the day you start writing your book." They immediately disappeared, and I did as I had been told—I got out of bed, went into my home office, and began writing *The Twisted Path*.

I also experienced an angel appearing as a messenger when our family's car went over a cliff on a snow-blinding day in Colorado. That morning, although weather conditions were almost blizzard-like, my husband and I decided to go snowmobiling as we were very accomplished at the sport. My younger daughter accompanied us, but my older daughter had a sore throat and stayed home with my mother-in-law. Not too long after we left the house my mother-in-law received a phone call telling her we had had an accident. She drove with my daughter to the crash site. Knowing the chances of our survival were not good, she advised my daughter to stay in the car. My daughter told me afterward that she had been sitting alone in the car frightened and crying, when someone appeared outside the back window and a voice said, “It’s okay. Don’t be frightened. Your mother will be fine.” Then the person disappeared. She said she had never before seen that person though we were familiar with most residents in the tiny town.

Another story, about the appearance of an angel to protect a person, was told to me by a man who visited my mother in hospice care, Chaplain Doyle. After I mentioned I was a spiritual healer, he related the following story: “My wife and I were on the way home from a perfect weekend at a B and B in Jefferson, Texas. It was a beautiful day for our motorcycle ride back to our home in Plano. As we entered the small town of Hawkins, a teenage boy driving a Jeep pulled out of a gas station, made a left turn onto the highway, and ran over us. My wife of only three months was killed instantly. My right leg was cut off below the knee, and I, too, was expected to die since I had lost a massive amount of blood.

“After I came out of a two-week coma, I asked each pastor who visited my hospital room, ‘Why did Lisa die but I’m still alive?’ The pastors said, ‘It must have been her time, but you still have a purpose to fulfill.’

"Once released from the hospital, I returned to Hawkins to thank the paramedics for saving my life. One of the paramedics said, 'I saw your accident and was there in fifteen seconds. When I arrived on the scene, there was an older black man with you. He stayed with you the whole time we worked on you until Life Flight flew you to the hospital. The Hawkins police wanted to start the investigation right then with the older black man because he was there so quickly, but no one could find him. He couldn't have driven off, because we had shut down the highway. Also, Hawkins is a small town, and we know everyone. We all decided he was your guardian angel.

"I then went to the Hawkins Police Station to thank the police for saving my life. The police said they had had a photographer on the scene, and I asked to see the pictures. I looked through thirty or more photographs, but there was no older black man in any of them. I knew in my heart that an angel had been watching over me and I had been saved that day. It changed my life. I felt I had lived because God's purpose for me was to help others. I am now in my third year of my new profession as a hospice chaplain." Chaplain Doyle, a devout Christian, had apparently experienced a loving, caring angel in the form of an older black man sent by God to protect him from death. The fact that professionals working to save his life witnessed Chaplin Doyle's guardian angel is evidence that an angel did protect the chaplain since it would have served no purpose for the policemen, firefighters, and paramedics to make up a story about the black man at the scene of the accident.

Chaplain Doyle learned from his personal experience how God allows angels and spirits to care for us and that he could be a Christian and also have spiritual metaphysical experiences. From that day forward, he embraced this spiritual metaphysical experience and integrated it into his Christian belief system to spread the peace and joy of God's love to those in hospice care facing death.

My own experiences with angels and spirit guides over the years have convinced me that some of the many different ways God shows his love for us daily are by sending angels and spirit guides to help guide, instruct, protect, and comfort people.

CHAPTER 13

Practicing Energy Healing

I began using spiritual energy for healing at an accelerated pace after my spiritual training started in Ruidoso. In the Baptist churches I attended as a child and young adult, the healing miracles performed by Christ as told in the Bible were the only ones mentioned in sermons. My father once told me about Pentecostal—or charismatic—churches that believed in hands-on healing, but I never attended any of those churches and didn't understand what this belief entailed. Whenever I personally needed healing, I prayed to God and Jesus for it or went to a medical doctor.

However, Jean, my spiritual mentor in Ruidoso in 1997, included in her daily instruction examples of energy healing, which she felt would increase the pace of my spiritual development. After she performed a Reiki session on me to familiarize me with the technique, I felt relaxed and peaceful, and I felt energy run through my body. Although I wanted to broaden my knowledge of metaphysical spirituality as quickly as possible, because of how I had been raised I was apprehensive about using my hands to aid someone's healing. I decided to research the Bible to see what God said about it, and found the following verse:

> "To another faith by the same Spirit, to another gifts of healing by the one Spirit." (*Revised Standard Version*, 1 Cor. 12.9)

I also did online research to become more familiar and comfortable with the practice before making a commitment to it. *Alternatives for Healing*, a holistic medicine resource directory, stated: "Energy Healing is a form of healing that manipulates, restores, or balances the flow of energy in the body. The energy is channeled through the practitioner to the client, helping remove energy deficiencies and blockages, which then activates the body's own natural ability to heal itself. Treatments may entail a combination of healing modalities including Reiki, Polarity Therapy, Craniosacral, Yuen Method, Pranic Healing, and others. Emphasis is often placed on solving emotional or spiritual problems, which have a profound effect in other areas such as physical health problems."[1]

Ultimately, I decided Reiki did not conflict with my religious beliefs, and I asked Jean to instruct me in the practice. As part of my training, I learned that Reiki, which

Dr. Mikao Usui, who studied in a Buddhist monastery, rediscovered at the turn of the century after a long, dedicated quest, is a holistic energy healing treatment that works on the body, mind, and spirit. Practitioners channel energy into patients that affects their physical, mental, and spiritual well-being. Jean told me that in the Western world the ancient healing method known as Reiki, described as Universal Life Energy, is derived from two Japanese words: *Rei*, which refers to the spiritual dimension and the soul, and *Ki*, which refers to the vital life force energy flowing through everything alive. Its basis is elemental earth energy.

Jean also explained that the Tera-Mai form of the modality was given to Kathleen Milner, a well-known teacher of Reiki, in a consciousness-raising experience. Tera-Mai allows all four elements—earth, fire, water, and air—to flow together, greatly enhancing a healer's potential. After completing three levels of instruction on Reiki from Jean, I received the Tera-Mai Reiki Master Certificate.

Before long I heard of a healer who taught another form of energy healing called Tera-Mai Seichem. I contacted her and traveled to her home in Sedona, Arizona, for additional classes. According to my Arizona teacher, Seichem is based on, and originated from, the same source as Reiki. The original Seichem energy was given to a man named Patrick Zeigler in a consciousness-raising experience while or after spending the night in the King's Chamber of the Great Pyramid of Egypt. After several concentrated classes in Arizona, I received the Tera-Mai Seichem Master Certificate.

The more my knowledge expanded, the more comfortable I felt with energy healing modalities and with performing energy healing on others. I began offering healing services, believing that using different modalities in combination would enhance my healing treatments. The normal modality of healing I had learned involved placing my hands at prescribed places above my clients' bodies. But one day when working on a client I heard Spirit tell me to place my hands above her forehead and touch her. I did as I was told. Then I began receiving messages from Spirit intended for her and told them to her. The client seemed pleased with the outcome, and I felt comfortable using the same method with future clients.

After more sessions, I began to see Spirit's blue healing energy come into the top of my head and run down my face, neck, chest, arms, and hands and into the bodies of clients. I also began to see energy flow throughout my clients' veins, tissues, bones, and muscles. Spirit then directed me to place my hands in the areas needing the most healing. Thereafter I performed healing treatments using whatever method Spirit dictated. Sometimes I felt a great deal of heat in my hands and sometimes not, which didn't concern me as long as the clients felt the healing energy running through them. Every time I worked with clients, I was in awe of the unbelievable images God allowed me to see.

Consideration of the source of this healing energy required me to again integrate my Christian beliefs and my knowledge about metaphysical spiritual processes.

According to Christianity, all healing comes from God and Jesus Christ since no human is capable of such a feat. For me to better integrate my religious beliefs with the metaphysical energy healing I witnessed, Spirit allowed me to experience a healing involving my mother.

In 1998, my mother had a bad fall at her retirement home in Dallas, cracking several bones in her back and irritating her fibromyalgia—a nerve disease that causes continuous muscular pain and restricts normal activity. In January 1999, I went to Dallas for her eighty-eighth birthday. When I arrived, she told me about her frustration at not feeling well enough to go to lunch or a movie to celebrate. She never had much opportunity to leave the retirement home since I lived out of town, and I knew she would be disappointed if our plans were canceled.

As I sat quietly in the chair next to her bed, I felt an impulse to try to give her energy. I placed my hands on her forehead and told her to relax, then I closed my eyes and began to whisper a prayer: "Lord, please help me. Allow energy to flow through my hands and into Mother's body. Please ease some of her pain. Lord, help her feel better so she can go with me today."

Within seconds, I felt heat under my palms and my hands begin to slightly sway back and forth on her forehead. I opened my eyes to look at her, wondering if she had caused the movement, but her eyes were closed, and she lay perfectly still. The rocking movement of my hands increased, making my body rock back and forth as well. I closed my eyes again and saw the flow of energy inside her head—her brain, her eye sockets, her blood vessels, her breathing passages—then inside her neck and back. After a few seconds, I saw the energy move down her body and pulsate in her lower back, abdomen, thighs, calves, and feet.

At precisely the moment the energy exited her feet, Christ appeared at the foot of the bed. He had brown wavy hair that hung to his shoulders and wore a long white robe. Standing with his arms spread wide and his palms turned upward, he moved slowly around the end of the bed and walked to my side. Gently, he then placed his hands on top of my hands, and we shared a moment's touch. My body swayed back and forth, and tears streamed down my face. I didn't want the experience to end, but I was exhausted.

"Lord, thank you. I don't want to stop, but I'm very tired," I said, gradually removing my hands from under his and stepping away. Christ, however, continued to stand by the bed with his hands on my mother's head as I wept. I went to the bathroom to wash my face then saw it was time for my mother to go to the dining room for lunch. I went back to her bedroom to wake her, hoping I would see Christ one more time, but he was gone.

"Mother, it's time for lunch," I said, gently touching her arm. At first she didn't respond, but then she opened her eyes, looked up at me, and replied, "I think I went to sleep. I can't believe I went to sleep as badly as I was hurting. I felt so relaxed I thought I was going to sink down inside the mattress. Let's have lunch. I think I can even go to a movie. Charlotte, I don't feel any pain anywhere."

Mother dressed in a lovely skirt and blouse with shoes and jewelry to match. We walked to the dining room and joined some of her friends already seated. She ate a hearty lunch and didn't complain about feeling pain. After our meal, we drove to a neighborhood theater to see a movie. Upon returning to the retirement home around 3:30 p.m., Mother suggested we invite my brother and cousin to join us for dinner. They arrived at 4:30 p.m., and we visited for almost an hour before heading off to a popular restaurant that specialized in fried catfish, then waited twenty to thirty minutes for a table. To my surprise, my mother never spoke of being in pain. We returned to the retirement home around 7:30 p.m., and my brother and cousin didn't leave until 9:30 p.m. Then my mother admitted to being tired but still made no mention of any pain. She went to bed at 10:30 p.m. and, upon waking up the next morning, commented on her restful night's sleep.

When I had placed my hands on my mother's head in the hope of giving her a few hours of relief from pain, Christ's appearance, I am convinced, was as much to help with the melding of my Christian and metaphysical spiritual healing beliefs as it was to help alleviate my mother's pain. During this incident, his loving touch on my hands affected me deeply, and I felt a part of his loving grace.

One day, after months of giving clients energy healing treatments and messages from their spirit guides and master teachers, I received a message from Spirit: "You are no longer to be called a psychic, or a Reiki or Seichem energy practitioner. You are to be called a spiritual healer." Aligned with this message were two important facts I emphasized to the clients with whom I worked: the healing may or may not be successful, as it is God who decides who will and will not be healed; and, if healing of their minds, bodies, or spirits does occur, it comes not from me but from God, who uses me as his tool to send healing energy into others—something Spirit had told me.

In today's society, energy healing is considered an alternative metaphysical modality, even though people may not understand how it works or may not believe in the practice. The International Center for Reiki Training in Southfield, Michigan, says, "Reiki can never cause harm because Reiki is guided by the God-consciousness. It always knows what a person needs and will adjust itself to create the effect that is appropriate for them. One never need worry about whether to give or take Reiki or not. It is always helpful."[2] Due to this and other lessons I learned in energy healing, I eventually became a vessel for Spirit to heal others through hands-on healing.

Though I no longer perform healings, I am still a strong proponent of the positive benefits of energy healing for those who suffer from a variety of illnesses. Further, I do not feel energy healing is in conflict with my Christian faith or relationship with God and Jesus. As long as the energy healer performing the treatment operates from a very high spiritual place and for the greatest good of the patient, it is a wonderful alternative and accompaniment to traditional healing methods.

CHAPTER 14

Supporting Children with Spiritual Gifts

After my spiritual journey and rebirth began in 1997, the teachings from my spirit guides encompassed all facets of life, including teachings about children with spiritual gifts. Since I was a child born with unusual talents and raised in a strict religious society, I think they wanted to reassure me that my childhood gifts were God-given and encourage others to accept their own spiritual gifts as talents to be used to benefit themselves and others in leading better lives.

My spirit guides taught me that we are born "open," with no preconceived ideas of what is real or not real, normal or not normal. We have the ability to see spirits and the other side, and, in childhood, often have imaginary playmates. My spirit guides also taught me that during our teenage years a veil begins to cover our eyes and we become more closely connected to the earthly dimension. Soon, caught up in a fast-paced world of technology, we forget to pay attention to metaphysical spiritual happenings around us. We begin to ignore or explain away unusual circumstances that may reflect spiritual phenomena. Our egos take over, and we become more concerned with ourselves—with what we want or how events affect us. By then, the innate metaphysical spiritual abilities we had as children have been diminished.

My own spiritual journey has made me keenly aware of other children like me whom God has blessed with spiritual gifts that continue past childhood. Many of these children have unusual experiences, like seeing movement or human forms, especially in their bedrooms, but are fearful if the spirits are sinister in nature. Children whose paranormal experiences are discovered by their parents or guardians may be accused of having overactive imaginations, or lying, or seeking attention. Often, because of lack of understanding of an adult to assist them with their abilities, they feel isolated and suffer in silence, especially while facing many additional pressures due to rapid changes. They may also be petrified that their friends will learn of their experiences and ridicule them or treat them as outcasts. Further, they may think they are weird or crazy, or, due to religious teachings, they will go to hell. All such fears can cause self-doubt and anxiety.

When my two daughters began discovering their metaphysical spiritual gifts, I had no knowledge of the spirit world other than my infrequent out-of-body incidents as a child and teenager. I paid no attention to anything spiritual because I was surviving the perpetual storms of daily life: working seven days a week as a real estate agent, dealing with an abusive relationship, pursuing societal interests, and being a mom. Because my awareness of spirits had taken a back seat to daily life, I lacked the ability to offer my girls much guidance about their spiritual gifts, although I tried to support them when they shared their discoveries so they would not feel alone with them as I had with mine while growing up. Knowing my children also experienced unusual occurrences gave me additional comfort regarding my own paranormal experiences in childhood. I believed it was one more sign indicating God's acceptance of the integration of Christian beliefs and metaphysical abilities.

Once my spiritual journey began in Ruidoso, I gained a much better understanding of my daughters' metaphysical experiences and was finally able to give them advice as well as share my similar experiences with them. My older daughter's unusual abilities surfaced when she was a teenager. She told me she often saw and felt someone race her up the staircase in our two-story house. She said she saw brilliant colors around people, bugs, and other living things. I had no explanation for these occurrences since I had not yet experienced this, though I told her of my fascination with her ability.

Later I learned in my studies in Ruidoso that the colors my daughter saw around all living things were called auras. My husband and I attended a psychic fair in Ruidoso, where a woman took our photos with what she called a

Kirlian camera, explaining that it captured the invisible field of energy surrounding a person or object. The colors in our photos, while specific to each of us, consisted of blues, greens, reds, yellows, oranges, whites, blacks, and violets. With the development of my gifts, I have been able to see subtle auras around people when giving readings or performing hands-on healings, but I have never been able to see the brilliant colors my daughter can see.

My older daughter never seemed afraid of her abilities—instead, accepting that she was different. I have witnessed her, as an adult, walking into a room, stopping abruptly, and saying, "Oh, hello," when I have seen no one in the room.

By contrast, when my younger daughter shared her ability to see and hear spirits, she believed she was delusional. I attempted to offer her solace by explaining that God gives people metaphysical gifts of seeing and hearing spirits, but my efforts failed. Eventually, she became so uncomfortable with her abilities that she refused to speak with me about them. Now, however, having heard me speak about communicating with spirits for twenty-two years, she no longer fears her gifts. When I visit her, I sometimes witness her conversing with spirits she calls "grandparents." If I venture into her space and start talking, she will say, "Mom, wait. I can't hear." My heart sings, for I know the grandparents love her and have only the best intentions for her.

Each of my daughters has a daughter, both of whom are also extremely gifted. My granddaughters know about my spiritual gifts and trust me to advise them. When I lived in Pagosa Springs, Colorado, I received a phone call in the middle of the night from my older granddaughter, who was living in Washington state. She said, "Grandma, there's a spirit in my room. If I tell my dad, he'll laugh at me. What should I do, Grandma? It scares me."

I told her to sleep with the light on and tell the spirit not to touch her. I gave her a protection prayer demanding that only spirits of the Christ Light appear in her space, advising her to say the prayer during the day and especially at night. I told her to call me if she got no results from the prayer, but she never did.

A year or two later when I asked her about the episode, she denied it had happened, saying, "I was mistaken." Although disappointed by her refusal to discuss the incident, I knew that her denial had been influenced by fear of her father's ridicule. Now, as an adult, she is more accepting of her spiritual gifts. She becomes a little anxious occasionally but is eager to learn as much as possible about her gifts and the spirits with whom she lives. Once in a while she will ask for my opinion about some unusual experience.

I remember when my younger granddaughter, at eight or nine months of age, sat on the living room floor of her mother's apartment staring into space and laughing at someone. When she became a preteen, her abilities increased considerably. Often she would call to say she saw or heard spirits, and felt their energy. Since she was truly gifted and I didn't want her to be afraid, I gave her a protection prayer and told her to say it several times a day. I also told her to stand in her power and control her environment, suggesting she try automatic writing to communicate with spirits, as I had when first beginning my spiritual journey.

When Don and I moved to East Texas and she came to live with us for a while, she told me about the spirits she saw in our house, saying, "Grandma, there's a spirit sitting in the black chair in the living room. There's also a spirit sitting in the flowery chair in the den."

"Did you recognize them?" I asked. "Did they say anything?"

"No. They're just sitting there," she insisted.

She also told me that when she went to bed at night a spirit would tuck her in and say good night, commenting, "The spirit is so sweet. It always tells me it loves me. Then it kisses me on the cheek. It's really cool." She said she couldn't see the identity of the spirit but wasn't afraid of its energy.

For my younger granddaughter, now a teenager, paying attention to the spirits surrounding her has been replaced with focus on her cell phone, girlfriends, and boyfriends. But with my reassurance she has learned to embrace her gifts. Occasionally, she calls me with a question, knowing that she can always talk with me if an experience is a little scary.

It is imperative for parents of spiritually gifted children to understand the phenomenon of cohabitation with spirits. Parents who do not comprehend spiritual gifts should at least have the strength to provide aid and encouragement so their children realize they are not crazy or delusional if they experience spiritual incidents. Parents who have a child they suspect is experiencing spiritual phenomena should understand that such things exist and talk to their child in a calm and supportive manner, asking if the child sees or hears people or is experiencing unusual events, encouraging them to describe visitors or unexplainable episodes. If their child describes something potentially harmful, they should immediately seek the help of a physic, medium, or spiritual healer. If their child describes a sweet and loving experience and shows no apparent fear, they should try not to exhibit anxiety. Regardless of the type of episode their child is experiencing, they should realize that it is important to protect their home and all those who reside in it. Further, they should say the protection prayers included in chapter 8 of this book.

As a spiritually gifted child and teenager, I lived in a home where experiences or actions deviating from the normal parameters of religious acceptance were regarded as sinful. If my family had instead offered unbiased and uncritical responses to problems, I might have had greater self-confidence and thus avoided some of the poor choices I made in my younger years. Having to hide my true identify from the society in which I lived diminished my self-esteem, making it impossible to live up to my full potential. Because of religious and societal influences, I was fifty-one years old before I learned I was, and had always been, okay in God's view. It is my wish that all children who experience budding metaphysical spiritual gifts learn to believe they are okay when they are still children, that they are God's creations when born, regardless of any metaphysical gifts they may have, and that this knowledge bolsters their self-confidence.

CHAPTER 15

Dealing with Guilt, Shame, and Forgiveness

Religious and family teachings about guilt, shame, and forgiveness have a great impact on people's feelings of self-worth and peace of mind. Thus, it is important to be aware of how these teachings affect us and how we can overcome any negative effects they might be having. Once guilt and shame are ingrained deeply in the psyche of young minds by religious or family teachings, they undermine feelings of being good enough and can lead to a lifelong experience of diminished self-esteem, affecting all their endeavors. In my own experience, the pastors of the churches my parents and I attended preached a lot about guilt, defined as remorse for having done something wrong. They said we were all guilty of something, all sinners. After years of accusations of guilt being drummed into my conscious and subconscious minds, it was instilled in me that I was supposed to feel guilty, regardless of whether or not I had done anything to justify the feeling.

Consequently, as a child, I felt guilty if I didn't want to go to church; I felt guilty if I pushed in front of a schoolmate in line; and I felt guilty if I had hateful thoughts against another child. Not knowing any better, I equated all my negative feelings with guilt. Guilt I felt regarding fighting between my parents turned into shame. Their words and actions caused me to feel embarrassment, unworthiness, and disgrace. I feared my friends would think I didn't deserve a happy home life; and I feared that if their parents knew of the violence in my home my friends would not be allowed to socialize with me.

The pastors of the churches I attended as a child also preached about forgiveness, saying that all we have to do to rid ourselves of guilt and shame is ask God and Jesus for forgiveness. But, unfortunately, praying and asking God for forgiveness did not eliminate my feelings of self-loathing.

As an older teenager, I was aware that church teachings about guilt continued to impact my thoughts, particularly when my boyfriend committed suicide. Not only did I blame myself, but my father and his parents convinced me I was guilty for his death. Due to this experience, my guilt feelings and fear of causing others mental or physical anguish negatively affected my decision-making in future romantic relationships.

As an adult, I sometimes said "yes" when the voices in my head screamed "no" and my heart knew a relationship was in opposition to what I wanted in my life. I didn't have the courage to reject relationships for fear of inflicting pain, thinking I was not worthy of greater self-fulfillment. As a result, in two marriages I became a battered wife and later suffered from battered wife syndrome, which, according to Merriam-Webster Dictionary, is "the highly variable symptom complex of physical and psychological injuries exhibited by a woman repeatedly abused, especially physically, by her mate." I felt I deserved every bad thing I endured.

When I did muster up the courage and strength to remove myself and my children from the home, no one understood why. Because I appeared outwardly to be a strong, independent woman who excelled in business and a career in real estate and hid the abuse occurring in my marriages, members of my community believed our family had a loving relationship. Many said, "But he's so good to you and the children, how could you do such a hurtful thing?" I knew differently, but the associated guilt made me question my decision.

The common denominator in all these events was guilt and shame associated with failing in relationships and thinking the failures were my fault. When I now reflect on the ridiculous decisions I've made regarding personal relationships with men, it is obvious to me that they were prompted by my feelings of inadequacy and self-loathing, with no thought of self-protection. At the time, I did not understand how to combat my fears, stand in my own power, and take care of my children and myself.

When I married my current husband, Don, my lack of self-worth persisted, reinforced by the demons of my childhood, my boyfriend's suicide, and failed marriages. However, Don, who was secure in his self-esteem, gave me the strength and courage to look those demons in the eye rather than fall into depression. I called him "my knight in shining armor," for he allowed nothing but positivity in our marriage. Yet despite the fact that I fought guilt and shame, I still could not fully forgive myself for past events. It was not until I began my spiritual journey in Ruidoso that Spirit taught me I had to forgive myself for past actions in order to live in freedom in the present and attain greater fulfillment in life.

My spiritual journey in Ruidoso helped me redefine my relationship with God and Jesus Christ. I discovered God loved me in spite of the regrettable decisions I had made in my life. New feelings of self-worth began to replace the self-loathing I had felt for fifty years. My daily communication with the spirit world taught me what my religious upbringing had not: that I had always been a worthy human being in the eyes of God and that even though I had made mistakes I could still forgive myself—a lesson of utmost importance for living a healthy emotional life with fulfilling relationships.

My spirit guides also taught me the importance of forgiving others' transgressions against me. Religious sermons and Bible scriptures address this matter, but only my spirit guides provided the explanations I needed to be able to forgive others. They have taught me that each individual on this earthly plane has been programmed differently, that sometimes unconscionable actions of others toward us are due to their upbringing or unsavory life experiences, and that it is not our place to judge them or condemn them but to forgive them and let God do the judging. At one time, I harbored hatred in my heart for those who had deceived, hurt, or abused me or my children. Though forgiving their deeds was not an easy task, I asked for God's assistance, and after many months my spirit guides helped me fully understand the impact of the hatred within me: that I was the one being hurt and not the perpetrator, and that my contemptible feelings toward perpetrators were keeping me from realizing a more spiritual existence. As a result of this understanding, my quest for self-forgiveness as well as the forgiveness of others soon became an integral part of my everyday life. I thanked God and my spirit guides for the knowledge and peace that allowed me to begin living a richer life of emotional freedom. As it says in the Bible: "Let all bitterness and wrath and anger and clamor and slander be put way from you, with all malice, and be kind to one another, tenderhearted, forgiving one another, as God in Christ forgave you." (*Revised Standard Version*, Eph. 4:31–32)

In a perfect world, the words guilt and shame would be removed from dictionaries, not used in church sermons, and eliminated from the rhetoric of parents engaged in educating their children. Only with the strength given us by the teachings of loving parents or spiritual angels and guides are we able to conquer our fears of not being good enough, so diminished self-worth does not negatively affect our lives.

Today I can say truthfully: "I love myself. I love the person I've become. I have made many mistakes in my life, but I did the best I could with the knowledge I had at the time." Teachings about guilt, shame, and forgiveness by my angels and spirit guides, along with religious teachings about forgiveness, have allowed me to accept my true value: I now know that I am worthy of happiness and respect, even with my human shortcomings.

CHAPTER 16

Achieving Resolution, Understanding, and Peace

Over the years, I have come to believe that the true purpose of organized religion has been lost. It seems to no longer provide solace for those in need and those wanting to communicate with God. I believe part of the reason the number of religious seekers has grown exponentially in the United States is that, because organized religion no longer fulfills their needs, people are looking for more satisfying belief systems or practices.

My dissatisfaction and psychological withdrawal from the Christian church began in childhood, making me a seeker extremely early in life. When I was growing up, my father had led me to believe preachers and priests were all-knowing experts when it came to heaven, hell, and all that lies in between. He gave me the impression they talked to God and knew what was best for us. However, after attending churches and listening to sermons throughout my youth, I came to believe preachers have no authority.

When I reached adulthood and could choose whether or not to attend church, I strayed from organized religion. I had a strong belief in the existence of God and Jesus Christ, but the behavior of many preachers and the actions of some parishioners had made me question if they worshiped the same God as me. The churches I had attended were of all faiths—Baptist, Methodist, Episcopal, Catholic, Presbyterian, Church of Christ, and Christian—but never had I found one that would allow me to worship God and Jesus without prejudice. When occasionally attending church services in recent years, I have preferred a Catholic church where I could kneel—if I chose—while communicating with God. Even though I do not agree with the teachings of Catholicism, the atmosphere of reverence in Catholic churches has brought me closer to the God with whom I prayed.

Today I question if any of today's preachers or priests have conversed with God and Jesus, or spirits of the Christ Light. I question if any have undergone abuse from parents or spouses, and had out-of-body experiences as a means of escape for emotional survival. And I question if any have had near-death experiences and seen the other side. Part of my discomfort with attending church is my aversion to preachers, who, lacking appropriate knowledge of worldly and otherworldly events, judge their parishioners and assail them with threats of hell.

Another aspect of my discomfort with Christianity, and organized religion in general, is its insistence on delving into commerce or interjecting its belief system into politics. Most of today's churches seem to care more about income and profitability than about healing injured souls. When Christ walked this earth teaching the unconditional love and forgiveness of God, I do not believe his intention was to exploit himself in political arenas. Further, although I believe many churches offer parishioners a safe environment for social gatherings, countless people I have known express excitement about attending Sunday services simply to hear gossip, seemingly enjoying the social aspect of the churches more than the emotional experience of worshiping God.

The current problems with Christianity are aptly described by the following quote from *The Urantia Book*: "Christianity is threatened by slow death from formalism, over-organization, intellectualism, and other nonspiritual trends (involvement in commerce and politics). So-called Christianity has become a social and cultural movement as well as a religious belief and practice."[1] On the other hand, millions of people feel their week isn't complete without attending a brick-and-mortar church with a preacher or priest standing behind a pulpit in a filled sanctuary telling them God and Jesus Christ love them, and they will not go to hell if they follow the rules of their faiths.

By no means do I believe organized religion, an integral part of life for thousands of years, is unimportant in our society. I recognize that many people feel they must have organized religion to function properly in daily life, and I agree that people should worship as they wish.

But the closed-mindedness of Christianity saddens me, because I feel Christians' lives would be greatly enriched by experiences of the metaphysical spiritual realm.

The knowledge I have gleaned in the last twenty-two years from countless spiritual metaphysical teachings of Christ, my spirit guides and master teachers, and God's other well-intentioned spirits has validated for me that it is okay to be a Christian and also embrace metaphysical spirituality and returned to me my feelings of self-worth. The reclaiming of my feelings of self-worth has been instrumental in achieving a new sense of empowerment to act in the name of God to help others. Since my discovery of metaphysical spirituality in 1997, I have acquired a personal empowerment that does not require my attending any brick-and-mortar church. Regardless of where my physical body is, I am in church every day, speaking with God, Jesus, and any spirit guides around me. There are no rules of engagement except that these guides be from the Light of Jesus Christ. And I do not need someone to intercede with them on my behalf, feeling I have the power to connect with them myself.

At the onset of my spiritual journey, I don't remember being taught personal love and self-forgiveness. I was taught the Golden Rule—"Do unto others as you would have them do unto you"—but I was not taught that I was worthy of my own love. From childhood into adulthood, I didn't like myself. I felt I was a caring person, but I lacked self-esteem. After being introduced to spirit guides of the Christ Light, the countless spirits who have become a part of my life, I now love and respect myself. I believe religious philosophy, dogmas, and teachings can make people feel inadequate, while metaphysical spirituality allows people to stand in their own power, to know who they are, and to be their true selves.

God has allowed me to know him and the loving spirits who have been by my side since birth. They have taught me that to have a relationship with God people do not have to choose between organized religion and personal spiritual pursuits. They have also taught me that individuals can be Christian yet have their Christian experience enriched by metaphysical spiritual modalities. One evening in Hollywood, California, for instance, Christ approached my father and said, "Go home and become a preacher," an instruction that led to my father becoming a Baptist minister and subsequently helping many other people in their religious endeavors.

Ultimately, I believe that my spiritual journey has allowed me to become an extension of God, which was my heart's yearning since my awareness of him as a child. In my view, being an extension of God is not like New Age notions of individuals being godlike. In an online article, an anonymous writer spoke of Oprah Winfrey's spiritual teacher as a New Age guru. The writer said that according to New Age beliefs everyone is God. I have also attended metaphysical conferences where speakers taught not to believe in duality and that each of us is God. However, when people have described my beliefs as New Age I have quickly corrected them, saying, "No. I am not New Age.

I am old age." I cannot say, "I am God." Rather, I believe there is one God, one Supreme Being, one Source and that I am an extension of him, a tool to be used by him.

I believe Jesus is the Son of God, a great teacher and healer put on earth to save us from ourselves; to give us something to believe in; to sustain us; and to die so that we may be cleansed of our sins. Even as an evolved spiritual healing intuitive, I continue to strongly believe that God and Jesus are real. I believe God is loving, kind, understanding, and, importantly, forgiving. I was raised a Christian and continue to be a Christian, but I believe I am now an enlightened Christian. I consider myself a metaphysical Christian. I know there is great knowledge beyond the pulpit. For me, God embraces the metaphysical spirituality as a way for individuals to enrich their faith and experience God's power and love through others who have been gifted by him.

Moreover, I believe my gifts were given to me by God, finding clarification in the following Bible scriptures:

> "As each has received a gift, employ it for one another, as good stewards of God's varied grace." (*Revised Standard Version*, 1 Pet. 4:10)

> "Having gifts that differ according to the grace given to us, let us use them: if prophecy, in proportion to our faith." (Rom. 12:6)

"If service, in our serving; he who teaches, in his teaching." (Rom. 12:7)
"And his gifts were that some should be apostles, some prophets, some evangelists, some pastors and teachers." (Eph. 4:11)

"So that you are not lacking in any spiritual gift, as you wait for the revealing of our Lord Jesus Christ." (1 Cor. 1:7)

"You said, 'Behold, the Lord our God has shown us His glory and His greatness, and we have heard His voice from the midst of the fire; we have seen today that God speaks with man, yet he lives.'" (Deut. 5:24)

The following passages, from *The Book of Knowledge* by J. J. Hurtak, further solidify my belief:

"The People of God will also receive five additional Gifts of the Holy Spirit when they are fully actualized. These will be the gifts of speaking in spiritual-scientific tongues; resurrecting the dead; speaking angelic languages; the ability to see and work with angelic teachers of Light in this world and the co-existing world . . . "[2]

"In addition, you are given spiritual Masters and Guides who will take you into other kingdoms, but

> they are your redeemers only in so far as they work with the Christ . . ."[3]

I believe God reaches out to people in a number of different ways—through psychics, healers, mediums, teachers, and preachers. People who are considered to truly possess spiritual metaphysical gifts are tools of God to help heal, comfort, and direct those who are in need and searching for greater spiritual understanding and to spread God's word. I believe God has put on earth many options—people with metaphysical gifts, traditional houses of worship, and various metaphysical spiritual modalities—so individuals may choose those that will best help them express their true selves.

I was told soon after beginning my spiritual exploration that the main reason I had walked through fire, starting in early childhood, was so I would have sincere compassion for, and understanding of, those who asked for my guidance. Many people have suffered from abuse, infidelity in their marriages, loss of loved ones, and other traumatic experiences. Because of the apparent contradiction between Christianity and metaphysical spirituality, some are afraid to ask for guidance to alleviate their suffering. When asked, "Will God be vengeful if I seek guidance or healing from a spiritual healer?" I have always answered, "No. God is the one who gives the guidance and performs healing. The spiritual healer is only a conduit of his loving grace."

Similarly, while doing readings and energy healings for clients, I began every session with a prayer asking for God's guidance. I then assured my clients that all information came from God or his loving spirits of the Light of Jesus Christ. I always felt the power and energy of Christ enter my body and my mind as I spoke with clients.

Blending Christianity and metaphysical spirituality has helped me overcome self-doubt and given me confidence to trust the voices inside my head and the feelings in my gut to guide me in the proper directions. Metaphysical spirituality has also allowed me to live my life without fear of retribution from a punishing God, so often described by men behind pulpits. It has allowed me to get rid of the demons and pain that filled my heart. Sad memories remain but have faded. The blending of my core Christian beliefs and metaphysical spirituality has given me joy for which I had no understanding until my spiritual quest began.

I believe that anyone who seeks a more gratifying life, to know their higher power, and to truly comprehend God's unconditional love is capable of attaining wisdom and joy by various means. As Ralph Waldo Trine writes his book *In Tune with the Infinite*:

> This mighty truth which we have agreed upon as the great central fact of human life is the golden thread that runs through all religions. When we make it the paramount fact in our lives we will find that minor differences, narrow prejudices, and all these

> laughable absurdities will so fall away by virtue of their very insignificance that a Jew can worship equally as well in a Catholic cathedral, a Catholic in a Jewish synagogue, a Buddhist in a Christian church, a Christian in a Buddhist temple. Or all can worship equally well about their own hearth-stones, or out on the hillside, or while pursuing the avocations of every-day life. For true worship, only God and the human soul are necessary. It does not depend upon times, or seasons, or occasions. Anywhere and at any time God and man in the bush may meet.[4]

The one constant in all religions is a God—a Higher Power, a Higher Source, a Supreme Being—regardless of the name by which it is called. As a follower of God, I believe it's okay with him to embrace spiritual metaphysical gifts, as he provides those gifts.

In fact, my greatest desire in life is to be as close as possible to God, Jesus Christ, and the lovely spirits who surround me. It is also my desire to help others understand that God loves us all regardless of who we are or what walk of life we travel. I want people to realize that it is okay for a Christian, or a member of any organized religion, to have metaphysical spiritual experiences, for I believe that God endorses any and all avenues to a more spiritual and fulfilling life.

NOTES

Chapter 7

1. Philip D. Kenneson, "What's in a Name? A Brief Introduction to the 'Spiritual but Not Religious,'" Liturgy 30, 3–13.

2. Robert Wuthnow, *After the Baby Boomers: How Twenty- and Thirty-Somethings Are Shaping the Future of American Religion* (Princeton, NJ: Princeton University Press, 2007), 112–135.

Chapter 11

1. Barbara Karnes, RN, *Gone from My Sight: The Dying Experience* (Vancouver, WA: Barbara Karnes Publishing, 2008), 5.

Chapter 12

1. J. J. Hurtak, *The Book of Knowledge: The Keys of Enoc*h, Key 117:56 (Los Gatos, CA: The Academy for Future Science, 2004), 163.

Chapter 13

1. Unknown, *Alternatives for Healing: A Leading Holistic and Alternative Medicine Resource Directory*, www.alternativesforhealing.com.

2. William Lee Rand, "How Does Reiki Work?" *Frequently Asked Questions* (Southfield, MI: International Center for Reiki Training, 1991), www.reiki.org.

Chapter 16

1. Unknown, *The Urantia Book* (Chicago, IL: The Urantia Foundation, 2005), 2,083.

2. Hurtak, *The Book of Knowledge*, Key 113:44, 127.

3. Hurtak, *The Book of Knowledge*, Key 117:56, 163.

4. Ralph Waldo Trine, *In Tune with the Infinite, The Life Books*, vol. 2 (San Bernardino, CA: Timeless Wisdom Collection, 2016), 185.

About the Author

Charlotte McGuire Goodwin is an ordained metaphysical minister and a spiritual metaphysical practitioner certified to engage in the treatment of physical and mental ailments and conditions through the use of Spiritual Mind Treatment. In addition to publishing *The Twisted Path*, her first book, she has been a contributing writer for online magazines and newsletters.

A spiritual healing intuitive, she has used her gifts of psychic mediumship, clairvoyance, clairaudience, and clairsentience in holistic spiritual counseling and vibrational energy healing. She holds master certifications in both Tera-Mai Reiki and Tera-Mai Seichem. In all her healing endeavors, she states that her gifts are derived from God.

Blessed since birth with spiritual gifts, Charlotte has been told that she is a conduit for the spirit world to channel healing to people; to give answers that provide comfort for those who suffer; to assist and direct those with a desire for spiritual awakening; and to help those in need of physical healing. Before devoting herself full time to her spiritual practice of helping others heal, she was a successful businesswoman, business owner, and community leader.

Charlotte and her husband, Don, currently live in San Miguel de Allende, Mexico.

Made in the USA
Monee, IL
20 August 2022